Waterfalls

of Virginia &
West Virginia

2ND Edition

174 Falls in the Old Dominion and the Mountain State

Randall Sanger

Adventure Publications
Cambridge, Minnesota

Dedication

To my beautiful wife Melissa and my precious daughter Hannah. I love you!

Disclaimer This book is meant as an introduction the waterfalls of Virginia and West Virginia. It does not guarantee your safety in any way—when visiting waterfalls, you do so at your own risk. Neither Adventure Publications nor Randall Sanger is liable for property loss or damage or personal injury that may result from visiting waterfalls. Before you visit a waterfall, be sure you have permission to visit the location, and always avoid potentially dangerous situations or areas, such as cliffs or areas with moving/deep water or areas where wildlife (snakes, insects) may be a concern. In particular, beware of slippery rocks, drop-offs, fast-moving or high water levels, and wilderness conditions. Your safety is your personal responsibility.

Cover photo: Randall Sanger
All photos by Randall Sanger
Edited by Brett Ortler
Cover and book design by Lora Westberg

10 9 8 7 6 5 4 3

Waterfalls of Virginia and West Virginia: A Guide to More Than 130 Waterfalls in the Great Lakes State
Second Edition 2018
Copyright © 2018 by Randall Sanger
Published by Adventure Publications, an imprint of AdventureKEEN
310 Garfield Street South
Cambridge, Minnesota 55008
(800) 678-7006
www.adventurepublications.net
All rights reserved
Printed in China
ISBN 978-1-59193-723-4 (pbk.); ISBN 978-1-59193-724-1 (ebook)

Acknowledgments

I have so many people to thank for helping make this book possible. My wife Melissa is amazing in her support of my work and puts up with all of my many absences. My awesome parents have always encouraged and supported me in my photography endeavors, and they have been a huge help to Melissa and me by watching our daughter Hannah while I am away or hard at work in my home office. Many thanks to Melissa's wonderful parents for their encouragement, and also for their help in watching Hannah for us.

Several family members have been instrumental in my waterfall photography pursuits over the years. Thanks to my Aunt Sue for taking me to the Cascades in Virginia years ago, and to my Uncle Raymond and Aunt Sarah for introducing me to West Virginia's Brush Creek Falls; it remains a favorite waterfall to this day. Thanks to my Uncle Bill for being my photography mentor and teaching me long-exposure techniques for waterfalls at Sandstone Falls.

Numerous friends, and even folks I have not met personally, have been instrumental in making this book, by scouting waterfalls for me, making me aware of new waterfalls they've found, hiking to waterfalls with me, sharing waterfall locations, and simply offering words of encouragement during this process. It's impossible to list everyone, but a special thanks goes to Kevin Akers for all of the help and company on the vast majority of the Virginia section. Thanks to Martin Radigan and George Fletcher for their help in the Northern Virginia region, and to John and Ruth Ann Bowman for their help and hospitality with the Piedmont region of Virginia. Thanks to Brent McGuirt for leading me to a couple Virginia waterfalls that I was unaware of. Thanks to Art Harvey for the company on numerous hikes in the New River Gorge regions and for leading me to a couple waterfalls that I was unaware of. Thanks to Curt Helmick and Mike Stump for all the scouts and company in the Mountain Lakes and Mountaineer Country regions of West Virginia. Thanks to Mike Carpenter, Rick Morrison, and Bobbie Swan for their tips on Valley Falls and Deckers Creek, as well as their company on a few hikes. Thanks also to Todd Williams for his friendship and constant encouragement. Thanks to my good friends "The Static Brothers" for the encouragement and for all the great times chasing waterfalls—several of the images in this book came from one of our trips. Many thanks to Fred Wolfe; I followed his steps to several of the waterfalls in the New River Gorge regions—some of which may still be unknown without his initial explorations. And a huge thank you to Ed Rehbein for all of his help and encouragement.

Lastly, thanks to all the great people who make up AdventureKEEN: Tim Jackson for reaching out to me to take on this project; Brett Ortler for all the great suggestions and advice during the editing process; and Lora Westberg. A big thank you goes to the followers of my social media accounts; your help in selecting a few of the photos for this book is greatly appreciated.

Preface

I'm not certain exactly when the waterfall bug hit me. Perhaps it was a trip to Ruby Falls in Tennessee as a toddler. Or when I was a child on family trips to my grandparents' as we drove by beautiful rivers and streams with cascading water. Or maybe it was as a young teen on a visit with my cousins to the Cascades in Virginia. Or quite possibly, it was as a young adult, while driving down the road to explore the ghost town of Thurmond and spotting Dunloup Creek Falls in my rearview mirror, then quickly abandoning the trip to Thurmond and doing a U-turn in the middle of the road to go back to admire and photograph what is still one of my favorite waterfalls.

Whenever it was, the bug hit hard. I've been captivated by falling water for many years, and I am to this day. The idea for this book was born years ago when I purchased the first edition of *North Carolina Waterfalls* by Kevin Adams. I thought to myself then that I would one day produce a similar book for the waterfalls of West Virginia. Life has a way of getting in the way of dreams, and I had to put my book idea on the back burner, but I still sought out and photographed West Virginia waterfalls at every opportunity. Several years later, Kevin published another book on waterfalls, but this one covered West Virginia and Virginia. I was disheartened: someone had beaten me to the punch, but at least an avid waterfall fan wrote it. I was encouraged, though, because while he covered a lot of territory, there were many waterfalls I had photographed that were not in his book. I truly felt that if I were to publish a WV waterfall book in the future, it would contain enough new material to have a place in the market.

In 2009 I received an email from a social media contact inquiring if I'd be interested in joining him in publishing a book on the waterfalls of West Virginia's New River Gorge. Of course I jumped at the opportunity, and in the fall of 2010, Ed Rehbein and I saw our labor of love in print. *West Virginia Waterfalls: The New River Gorge* went on to win several awards, and we both still receive great comments about it to this day.

But I still wanted to produce a book on West Virginia waterfalls and continued to jot notes and look for new waterfalls as time allowed. Fast forward to November 2015, and I'm answering an email from AdventureKEEN about the possibility of authoring another edition of *Waterfalls of Virginia and West Virginia!* The cool thing about this is that Kevin Adams was unable to take on the project and is the person who recommended me to the publishing company. Funny how things work out. Not only have I been able to put together a book on my West Virginia waterfalls, but I was given the opportunity to explore the beautiful state of Virginia and chase the many waterfalls in that state as well.

I hope you enjoy this book and use it to discover the beautiful waterfalls of Virginia and West Virginia. I've included a few tips and suggestions from my years of photographing waterfalls and leading photography workshops that I trust you will find helpful.

Enjoy the chase, and safe travels!

Table of Contents

Virginia Waterfalls

Introduction

From water thundering down hundreds of feet to the smallest, intimate cascade, waterfalls are special. We are drawn to falling water for the beauty, wonderment, and respite it provides.

In this book, I share with you over 150 waterfalls; 75 in each state are prominently featured, and for good measure, I throw in a dozen more selections at the end of each state's section. Obviously, this is not an exhaustive compilation of Virginia and West Virginia waterfalls. Each state has hundreds to choose from, but here I have simply shared with you a selection of the top waterfalls each state has to offer. While I have seen close to 300 in West Virginia and over 100 in Virginia, there are just too many waterfalls for a book of this size, and there are still quite a few I have yet to see. And, as more and more private land opens up and becomes available for exploration, I'm sure I'll have plenty more to share with you in future editions.

If you visit every waterfall in this book, you will hike close to 200 miles, drive on three scenic highways (Virginia's Skyline Drive and Blue Ridge Parkway, West Virginia's Highland Scenic Highway), hike on the famed Appalachian Trail, walk on three historic rail-trails, visit national parks and forests, state parks, forests, and wildlife management areas, and county and city parks, see historic grist mills, and you might even ride a scenic-excursion train. Several hikes will have you deep in the backcountry, miles from civilization, while other waterfall treks will have you among the hustle and bustle of metropolitan areas.

There is a great mix of roadside waterfalls, short hikes, and long hikes throughout the book. The longest hike is in West Virginia, to the High Falls of the Cheat, while there are several long hikes in Virginia's Shenandoah National Park. In fact, most of your longer hiking distances will be in the state of Virginia. West Virginia has a greater concentration of roadside beauties or short waterfall hikes, and a few fun-to-downright-scary bushwhacks.

How to Use This Book

This book prominently features 75 waterfalls in Virginia and 75 waterfalls in West Virginia, with each state divided into regions. For an overview map with all of the falls, see page 18 for Virginia and page 128 for West Virginia.

Within each state's region, the falls are featured according to three general categories: Top 10, Must-See, and More Waterfalls. Naturally, the Top 10 Falls are what I consider the 10 best waterfalls in each state, mostly due to their sheer beauty, but also due to consistent water flow and other factors. Each Top 10 waterfall will be featured on four pages, with a two-page photo spread followed by two pages of information. The Must-See Falls are also prominently featured with a full-page photo and a full page of information. In some instances, a stream with multiple waterfalls will be collectively categorized as a Top 10 or Must-See. The waterfalls in the More Waterfalls category receive a little less exposure, but they are still quite beautiful. Lastly, see page 126 for 12 More Virginia Waterfalls to Explore and page 262 for 12 More West Virginia Waterfalls to Explore; these 24 waterfalls just didn't quite make the cut for more recognition, but they are certainly worth seeking out if you're in the general area.

Each waterfall account will be accompanied by a color photo. Some guidebooks are heavy on the info, while the photographs leave a lot to be desired, if there's a photograph at all. We wanted to provide you with great photography in addition to all the information you'll need to find the waterfall. I've tried to select images that offer a good sense of place, so that you'll know what to expect before you arrive.

The following information is included for each waterfall in the three main categories:

Location: Where the waterfall is located; typically, this is the park or natural area where you'll find the waterfall. An approximate location is marked on the map of each state on pages 18 and 128. Nearly all of the waterfalls in this book are on public land. The waterfalls on private property are accessible either by paying a fee or at no charge through the graciousness of the landowner. Lastly, I've featured some waterfalls that can be viewed from public roads, but the waterfalls are on private property and should not be approached. Please respect the rights of the landowners and do not trespass.

Address/GPS for the Falls: Sometimes there will be a physical street address for the falls. More often than not, the address will be of the park, and in some instances, simply the name and/or route number of the road. The GPS coordinates are for the location of the waterfall itself, not a parking area or street address, so don't expect to be able to just plug these coordinates into your car or phone and drive right to the waterfall (unless it's at a roadside location).

Directions: General driving directions to the parking area and/or trailhead used to access the waterfall.

Website: If available, I'll list a website of the waterfall, or in some instances, the website of the park where the waterfall is located.

Waterway: The river or stream that generates the waterfall.

Nearest Town: The nearest town/city.

Height: The approximate height of the falls.

Crest: The width of the falls; since this fluctuates greatly due to the seasons and rainfall patterns, I usually use the word "varies."

Hike Difficulty: Easy to strenuous, and I'll tell you why.

Trail Quality: Details about the trail surface, obstacles to expect, and ease of navigation.

Round-Trip Distance: The distance you'll hike from your car or trailhead to the falls and back.

Admission: While this doesn't apply in West Virginia, several of the Virginia waterfalls are located in parks that charge entrance or parking fees. I'll list those fees here. If you visit one of the waterfalls in a Virginia Wildlife Management Area, please note that anyone 17 and older who wants to access a Virginia Wildlife Management Area must purchase an Access Permit unless they possess a valid Virginia hunting, freshwater fishing, or trapping license, a valid Virginia boat registration, or are otherwise waived from the requirement. The cost for the Daily Access Permit is $4 per person. The cost for the Annual Access Permit is $23 per person and both prices include the $1 per transaction license agent fee. tinyurl.com/accessfee

Trip Report & Tips: A firsthand account of my visit(s) to the waterfalls, followed by directions to reach the falls. In a lot of the accounts, I'll share some personal insight on good vantage points from which to photograph the waterfall. I'll mention possible hazards to be aware of or the best times to visit. And, if there is a nearby waterfall not featured elsewhere in the book, I'll make you aware of that as well. In some instances, I'll share historical or fun facts about the waterfall or the general area.

The Waterfalls of the Two Virginias

While the two states are quite similar, especially in the mountainous regions, the waterfalls in each state are strikingly different. Virginia has several waterfalls hundreds of feet high, while the tallest waterfall in West Virginia is less than 100 feet high. You'll find a lot of slide-type waterfalls in Virginia, but in West Virginia there are few slides to be found. Travertine buildup is common around Virginia waterfalls, but I've seen no travertine in West Virginia. No matter their differences, there is one definite similarity: the waterfalls of the two Virginias are beautiful and worthy of protection and preservation.

About the Regions

I've divided each state into regions so that you'll be better able to plan your waterfall excursions. In Virginia, to avoid confusion, I've followed preestablished regions used by other guidebook authors. Those regions are Southwest Virginia, Valley and Ridge, Blue Ridge Parkway and Vicinity, Shenandoah National Park, Piedmont, and Northern Virginia. The Southwest region offers the most waterfalls in Virginia, with the Piedmont region having the fewest.

In West Virginia, I've loosely followed suit with travel regions first used by the WV Division of Tourism. Those regions are Upper New River Gorge and Bluestone River Tributaries, Central New River Gorge, Lower New River Gorge and Gauley River Tributaries, Mountain Lakes, Blackwater Falls State

Park, Potomac Highlands, and Mountaineer Country. Since there are so many waterfalls in the New River Gorge region, I felt it best to break those up into three regions, much like they are divided in my and Ed Rehbein's book *West Virginia Waterfalls: The New River Gorge*. And while Blackwater Falls State Park is in the Potomac Highlands region, there are some magnificent waterfalls in the park, and I felt they deserved their own region/chapter.

Lastly, while the waterfalls are separated into regions, they aren't necessarily in geographic order within the regions. Instead, the order of the waterfalls is driven by the various rankings of the falls. To find waterfalls near you, consult the maps (page 18 for VA, page 128 for WV) and then turn to the corresponding page numbers.

Photographing Waterfalls

I've been chasing waterfalls and capturing images of them for many years. I particularly enjoy using long exposures to achieve a nice silky look on the water. Each waterfall will have its own personality and characteristics, with water flow, cloud cover, and seasonal variations combining to allow you to capture the best image possible that day. The following are a few tools you'll need to photograph waterfalls:

Camera—I strongly recommend at least a basic DSLR camera if you're serious about making quality waterfall images. While you might sometimes make a good image with a point-and-shoot camera or a cell phone, it's going to be hard to do it consistently. Some advanced point-and-shoot models do offer the ability to change f-stops and ISO speed, but not to the degree I prefer. A DSLR offers you the ability to have complete control over an image; it also allows you to switch lenses, and add filters that block light for longer exposures and/or to eliminate harsh glare.

Tripod—A sturdy tripod is a must for waterfall photography, especially for long exposures. It's almost impossible to achieve a sharp image by hand-holding during an exposure of 1/60th of a second or longer. Since you'll be hiking a lot, a lightweight but strong carbon-fiber tripod is your best bet, but less expensive aluminum tripods are sufficient. Keep in mind that you'll be on very uneven terrain, so a tripod with independent leg movement is ideal.

Circular Polarizing Filter–Another must for photographing waterfalls is a circular polarizing filter. First, the circular polarizing filter blocks a stop or two of light, allowing those longer exposures you'll want. But more importantly, by rotating the outer ring of the filter, you'll be able to eliminate or enhance reflections, eliminate harsh glare on wet rocks and other surfaces, and boost the saturation of the image.

Neutral Density Filter–These filters come in various degrees of density to block light from entering your camera. I typically carry a 3-stop neutral density filter in case I need a little more light blocked than what my circular polarizing filter is blocking. But then I stack my circular polarizing filter on the neutral density filter so that I will still reap the benefits of using the circular polarizing filter. Of all the photos featured in this book, I only used the circular polarizing and neutral density filter combination twice, and that was to gain a long enough exposure to accentuate swirling water. More often than not, the circular polarizing filter will be all you need to make dramatic waterfall images.

Cable Release/Remote/Built-In Timer–When you press your shutter button, you introduce vibration. To eliminate this, connect a cable release to your camera and use it to trip the shutter. Wireless remotes work great as well, or simply use the 2-second timer built into your camera.

And now, a few tips about photographing waterfalls:

ISO Speed–Digital cameras are designed to approximate the ISO speed of film cameras. Typically, the lowest ISO setting on digital cameras is 100, but some cameras offer lower ISO speeds. For what it's worth, I normally use an ISO speed of 50. The lowest ISO setting is best for waterfall photography, as it will introduce less noise and provide great sharpness, detail, color accuracy, and longer exposure times.

F-Stop–For the long exposures you're after, and to obtain maximum depth of field, you'll want to use an f-stop around the range of f-11 through f-22. Of course, the type of light you're faced with, and the volume of water flow, will dictate a lot of your choices for you. I typically shoot at f-16, as this f-stop is the sharpest with the lens I use. If you're faced with a raging torrent, you may need to go to f-11 or f-9 for shorter exposures, so that you'll maintain detail and texture in the water.

Composition—A quality composition turns a snapshot into a great shot. A strong foreground is key, with leading lines that draw the eye through the frame. More often than not when photographing a waterfall, you can use large rocks or boulders found in the stream as your foreground subject. Sometimes, cascading water rushing through the lower portion of the frame is perfect for your foreground.

Whether I'm shooting alone, with friends, or leading my photography work-shops, I like to remember three things that help me obtain great compositions. The first is to **Get Low**. Change your point of view or perspective of the scene by getting low to the ground. Sometimes this offers better compositions, sometimes it doesn't, but at least give it a try. Next is to **Get Wide**. An extreme wide-angle lens greatly enhances my creative compositions, especially with waterfalls. A wider angle of view offers a much better sense of place, and you'll be able to move closer to the waterfall to obtain composi-tions you wouldn't get with a standard zoom. That doesn't mean you should leave your telephoto lens at home, though; I love using my longer lenses to isolate certain sections of the waterfalls. However, an extreme wide-angle lens (think 11–16mm for crop-sensor bodies or 16–35mm for full-frame cameras) should typically be your go-to lens for waterfall photography. Lastly, you need to **Get Wet**. Often, the best shot of a waterfall will be from within the stream itself, or on the other side of the stream. I've made some very unique images from heavily visited waterfalls simply by getting wet. Of course, getting wet does carry some risk, and I'll cover that soon.

Avoid Blue Sky Days—Waterfall photography is best under a good deal of cloud cover. In fact, I prefer shooting just after a rain or during a light rain, so that the entire scene is balanced with everything nice and wet. Dry rocks are a distraction, so if I am shooting on a dry day, I try to splash all the rocks I can safely splash. Harsh light on a waterfall is an image killer, so avoid shooting on sunny days if at all possible. On dark, overcast days, you can realistically shoot waterfalls from sunup to sundown. On days that lack adequate cloud cover, you'll obviously want to visit the waterfalls in the early-morning or late-afternoon hours, when the sun is not shining on the waterfall or its surroundings.

Waterfall Safety

Chasing waterfalls carries a degree of risk. It involves scrambling down steep hillsides, walking along slick creek banks, or even wading into the stream, all to capture that perfect shot. Some waterfalls will have barriers in place to keep us safe, while other waterfalls have no such restraints. Regardless, you need to use common sense around waterfalls. It's certainly tempting to go near the top of a waterfall, but just don't do it. It's not worth it. Every year, people fall to their deaths because they were too close to the edge of a waterfall.

While I mentioned earlier that sometimes it's best to Get Wet for better compositions or vantage points, common sense again dictates not to enter a stream with swift currents. For example, Great Falls in Virginia is notorious for deadly undercurrents, so please, stay out of fast-moving water.

Move with care when you're around waterfalls. Slick surfaces are everywhere, and it's very easy to take a step and, before you know it, you've fallen. Trust me, I've had my fair share of falls due to not paying attention, or even when I thought I was paying attention. More often than not, wet and/or algae-covered rocks will get you, but sometimes there are other issues at play. For instance, at Douglas Falls and a few others in West Virginia, rocks are coated with some sort of funk due to acid mine drainage and the resulting cleanup measures. These rocks are slippery even when dry, and they're like walking on ice when wet, so be very careful and slowly inch your way along until you're sure of your footing.

Lastly, in Virginia and West Virginia, there are animals and reptiles that could make your waterfall hike a bad experience. Black bears are native to both states, and I've seen them primarily in Virginia's Shenandoah National Park and in West Virginia's Potomac Highlands Region. I typically carry bear spray with me, just in case, but in all my years of hiking, the bears have always moved on when encountered.

Copperheads and rattlesnakes are common in both states, and Virginia also has the cottonmouth, and I've seen them while hiking in both states. Each time, the snake retreated when it saw me, but do be aware of your surroundings, and make sure you're careful and watch where you place your hands when using boulders and ledges to steady yourself as you scramble down to a waterfall.

I've been stung by bees, bugs, nettle, and more while hiking, so keep in mind that there are insects and plant life that can make your excursion uncomfortable. I always have bug spray in my pack and will sometimes use a permethrin spray for my clothes to protect myself from ticks and other insects. You'll also be walking on a lot of uneven terrain with loose rocks and exposed roots, so be careful not to twist an ankle or worse as you're hiking.

With all that said, if you're careful and stay alert to your surroundings, you'll have a most wonderful experience as you visit the waterfalls of the two Virginias.

Waterfall Names

Several of the waterfalls in this book were named long ago, while others have no names. I took the liberty of naming a couple of them, but usually I kept with the regional practice of naming the waterfalls based on the name of the stream that produces them.

Map of Virginia's Waterfalls

Southwest

1. The Devil's Bathtub (p. 20)
2. The Falls of Little Stony (p. 24)
3. The Falls of Tumbling Creek (p. 28)
4. Crab Orchard Branch Falls (p. 32)
5. Corder Hollow Falls (p. 32)
6. Falls of Logan Creek (p. 34)
7. Big Falls (p. 34)
8. Big Rock Falls (Whitetop Laurel Falls) (p. 36)
9. Straight Branch Falls (p. 36)
10. The Chute (p. 38)
11. Cabin Creek Cascade (p. 38)
12. Lower Cabin Creek Falls (p. 40)
13. Middle Cabin Creek Falls (p. 40)
14. Upper Cabin Creek Falls (p. 42)
15. Wilson Creek Falls (p. 42)
16. Fox Creek Falls (p. 44)
17. Comers Creek Falls (p. 44)
18. Chestnut Creek Falls (p. 46)
19. Falls of Dismal (p. 46)

Valley and Ridge

20. The Cascades (p. 48)
21. The Upper Cascades (p. 52)
22. Falling Spring Falls (p. 56)
23. Stiles Falls (p. 60)
24. Roaring Run Falls (p. 62)
25. Roaring Run Slide (p. 64)
26. Double Falls on Roaring Run (p. 64)
27. Waterfall at Falls Ridge (p. 66)
28. Mill Creek Falls (p. 66)
29. Lace Falls (p. 68)
30. McGuirt Falls (p. 68)
31. Folly Mills Falls (p. 70)
32. Mill Creek Falls (p. 70)

Blue Ridge Parkway and Vicinity

33. St. Mary's Falls (p. 72)
34. Crabtree Falls (p. 76)
35. Apple Orchard Falls (p. 80)
36. White Rock Falls (p. 84)
37. Box Spring Falls (p. 84)
38. Wigwam Falls (p. 86)
39. Panther Creek Falls (p. 86)
40. Upper Statons Creek Falls (p. 88)
41. Lower Statons Creek Falls (p. 88)
42. Fallingwater Cascades (p. 90)
43. Bent Mountain Falls (p. 90)

Shenandoah National Park

44. Overall Run Falls (p. 92)
45. The Falls of Whiteoak Canyon (p. 96)
46. Dark Hollow Falls (p. 102)
47. Waterfalls on Cedar Run (p. 106)
48. Lands Run Falls (p. 108)
49. Hazel Falls (p. 108)
50. Upper Rose River Falls (p. 110)
51. Lower Rose River Falls (p. 110)
52. Lewis Falls (Lewis Spring Falls) (p. 112)
53. South River Falls (p. 112)
54. Upper Doyles River Falls (p. 114)
55. Lower Doyles River Falls (p. 114)
56. Jones Run Falls (p. 116)
57. Big Branch Falls (p. 116)

Piedmont Region

58. Falls of the Nottoway (p. 118)
59. Falls of the James (p. 118)

Northern Virginia

60. Great Falls of the Potomac (p. 120)
61. Scott's Run Falls (p. 124)
62. Piney Run Falls (p. 124)

● Top 25　● Must-See　● Other

The Devil's Bathtub

A must-see geological feature!

Devil Fork Slide

The Devil's Bathtub

What was once an area known mainly by area residents exploded in popularity a few years ago via social media. Visit for yourself and you'll understand why it is so popular. You'll need to arrive early in the morning to avoid a packed parking lot.

LOCATION: Jefferson National Forest

ADDRESS/GPS FOR THE FALLS: Devil's Fork Loop Trail; 36° 48.779′ N, 82° 39.041′ W

DIRECTIONS: From Dungannon, follow VA-65 South/VA-72 South for just under 8 miles to a right turn onto VA-619. Follow for 4.4 miles, and turn left and almost immediately cross a bridge. Follow for around 0.2 mile, then turn left at an abandoned white house and proceed a little over 0.2 mile to the parking area. Please note, the final 0.1 mile of the road to the parking area is full of holes and heavily rutted; proceed with caution if not in a high-clearance vehicle. There is no legal parking if you can't proceed.

WEBSITE: tinyurl.com/vabathtub

WATERWAY: Devil Fork

HEIGHT: A 10-foot cascading run leading to an amazing geological feature

CREST: Varies

NEAREST TOWN: Fort Blackmore

HIKE DIFFICULTY: Moderate to strenuous, depending on the water level at stream crossings

TRAIL QUALITY: Rocky, with exposed roots and numerous stream crossings

ROUND-TRIP DISTANCE: 4 miles

ADMISSION: None

TRIP REPORT & TIPS:

The Devil's Bathtub—the highlight of the Devil's Fork Loop Trail—exploded onto the scene a few years ago after being featured by websites such as The Weather Channel and reddit.

With little elevation gain, the hike isn't difficult, but numerous stream crossings can be tricky in higher water situations. My first trip was after a couple days of rain, and I made those stream crossings in water up to my thighs. The water was too high to actually see the Bathtub that day, so I enjoyed photographing the waterfalls above and below the Bathtub. I returned a few weeks later so that I too would have the quintessential Devil's Bathtub images.

The full trail is a lollipop loop and longer than listed here. I'm only detailing the shortest route to the Devil's Bathtub. From the parking area, climb the steps and bear left, and after walking a little over 0.2 mile, you'll reach the first stream crossing. This will be a good gauge for you to determine if you wish to keep going, as there are at least 10 more stream crossings. Soon after the crossing, you'll reach a junction at a trail sign. Turn left at the sign, and follow the yellow-blazed trail about 1.5 miles to a large swimming hole and waterfall. Make one more stream crossing, climb up the bank, and then scramble down a short spur path to see the Bathtub. Recent trail work and blazing has made the path easy to follow, and the stream crossing junctions are easy to recognize. If you're there when the water level is high, hike on up the trail about a half mile to see Corder Hollow Falls (page 33). Please note that the parking area is small, and no alternate parking sites are available. Due to the popularity of the hike, the area is often overcrowded, and parking cannot be found. If you find the parking lot full, don't contribute to the overcrowding by parking illegally. Simply return another day, and while you might be disappointed, your time certainly won't be wasted, as there is plenty to see in the area.

Upper Falls of Little Stony

The Falls of the Little Stony

LOCATION: Jefferson National Forest

ADDRESS/GPS FOR THE FALLS: Little Stony National Recreation Trail; Upper Falls: 36° 52.266' N, 82° 27.717' W; directions to the other falls follow

DIRECTIONS: From Coeburn, at the intersection of US-58 ALT and VA-72, follow VA-72 South for 3.4 miles, then turn right on VA-664/Corder Town Road. Follow for 1.1 miles, then turn left onto Forest Road 700 and follow for 1.3 miles, and then turn left onto Forest Road 701. Follow for 0.8 mile to the Falls of Little Stony parking lot.

WEBSITE: tinyurl.com/littlestonyva

WATERWAY: Little Stony Creek

HEIGHT: Upper Falls: 25 feet; Middle Falls: 12 feet; Lower Falls: 30 feet

CREST: Varies

NEAREST TOWN: Coeburn

HIKE DIFFICULTY: Easy, with some moderate scrambles down to stream level

TRAIL QUALITY: Good, but with some exposed roots and rocky areas

ROUND-TRIP DISTANCE: 1 mile

ADMISSION: None

TRIP REPORT & TIPS:

I became aware of the Falls of Little Stony several years ago. With my dog Rocky along for the ride, I finally took the time to check out the Falls of Little Stony on a surprisingly warm January day. From the moment I saw the first waterfall, I wished I had visited much sooner. The trail gently descends on an old narrow-gauge railroad bed into a gorge full of rhododendron and hemlock, paralleling and crossing Little Stony Creek along the way. The waterfalls are all impressive, with each having a neat personality and characteristics that make it easy to spend the day photographing here. The ease and short duration of the trail make this a great hike for families with small children, and I'm looking forward to bringing my wife and daughter here soon.

From the trailhead parking, follow the trail downstream, and in about 300 yards you'll reach a footbridge over Little Stony Creek with a view of the Upper

Middle Falls of Little Stony

Upper Falls of Little Stony

TRIP REPORT (CONTINUED): Falls. Continue on the trail a short distance to a spur trail to the left with a series of stone steps leading down to the base of the Upper Falls. Here you'll see the free-falling water plunging into a beautiful green pool. If you can pull yourself away from the falls, head on back up the steps and continue down the trail to the Middle Falls.

From the Upper Falls, follow the trail a few hundred yards downstream, cross the footbridge, and look for a short spur trail down to the stream, where you'll find the best vantage points for photographing the Middle Falls.

The Middle Falls is my personal favorite of the three. I'm a big fan of small waterfalls with unique traits and a cascading stream rushing away from the falls—the Middle Falls has all that. Surrounded by the lush greens of rhodo-dendron lining the banks, Little Stony Creek drops over a multisectioned ledge and immediately begins a cascading run downstream. This is where I decided I was going to get wet, and I entered the stream to capture water flowing over and around small boulders and rocks, with the Middle Falls in the background. I typically don't like placing man-made objects in my waterfall images, but here and at the Upper Falls, the footbridges spanning the creek really add to the scene.

Continue on the trail down to the Lower Falls. About 0.1 mile from the Lower Falls, the trail becomes a bit steeper, and you'll have to deal with some exposed roots. There is a nice viewing platform above the Lower Falls, but a short, steep spur trail on the opposite side of the platform affords you access to the stream. Of the three falls, the Lower Falls was my second favorite, mainly due to the cascading stream leading away from the falls. Water fanning over a jutted section of the streambed lured me back into the creek, and it was here that my dog was overcome with the desire to get wet as well. The Lower Falls is a typical stair-step fall, with a large, deep pool at the base. I haven't been here in the summer months, but I imagine the pool here and the one at the Upper Falls are popular swimming holes. If you haven't visited the Falls of Little Stony, add it way up high on your list; you won't be disappointed. I'll be going back often, so be sure to say hello if you see me there.

The Falls of Tumbling Creek

LOCATION: Clinch Mountain Wildlife Management Area

ADDRESS/GPS FOR THE FALLS: Tumbling Creek Road; Upper Falls: 36° 56.006′ N, 81° 49.602′ W; directions to the other waterfalls follow

DIRECTIONS: Via I-81, take the Chilhowie exit (exit 35) and follow VA-107 North for a little over 8 miles. Turn left onto East Main Street, and in 0.2 mile, turn right onto Allison Gap Road for 1.4 miles. Turn left onto Poor Valley Road and follow for 3.8 miles, then turn right onto VA-747/Tumbling Creek Road. Follow for about 4.8 miles to the Upper Falls. Due to the narrow roadway, I found it best to park at the Upper Falls and walk the short distance downstream to the other falls.

WEBSITE: tinyurl.com/clinchmountainva

WATERWAY: Tumbling Creek

HEIGHT: Upper Falls: about a 7-foot drop followed by a couple smaller cascades; Big Falls: 10 feet; Unnamed Cascade: about a 5-foot drop followed by a few smaller cascades; Twin Hollow Falls: two 12-foot drops converge into a cascading stream

CREST: Varies

NEAREST TOWN: Saltville

HIKE DIFFICULTY: Roadside views available; however, all are best viewed via short, but steep and rocky, scrambles down to the creek

TRAIL QUALITY: Easy roadside views, or rocky and steep scrambles down to the creek

ROUND-TRIP DISTANCE: 0.6 mile from roadside view of Upper Falls down to roadside view of Twin Hollow Falls and back

ADMISSION: See page 11 for details

TRIP REPORT & TIPS:

Writing this book presented me with the wonderful opportunity to explore the state of Virginia and the time to spend with one of my best friends. Kevin resides in Virginia with his son Austin, and they welcomed me into their home on several occasions as I worked on the book. Kevin made the time to go on many of the Virginia waterfall excursions with me, and his pretrip planning proved invaluable. Our visit to Tumbling Creek was the final stop of a two-day excursion that saw us hiking several miles along some beautiful trails and

Big Falls

Tumbling Creek Cascade

Twin Hollow

TRIP REPORT (CONTINUED): photographing eight waterfalls. We both agreed that Tumbling Creek was not only the highlight of that particular trip but was the star attraction among several previous excursions.

The Upper Falls is a classic multitiered shelf cascade in a remarkable setting. In the spring, surrounded by the new greens, it is simply hard to beat. I'm looking forward to checking out Tumbling Creek during the fall foliage season as well.

You should be able to see Big Falls as you drive up the road, and as mentioned in the directions, I'd suggest driving a short distance more and parking at the Upper Falls, as the parking is a bit more generous there. From the road, you can drop down to the base of the falls on a couple well-worn paths. I spent a lot of time here photographing from every conceivable angle.

If the Upper Falls and Big Falls haven't been enough to get you excited about Tumbling Creek, perhaps this unnamed cascade will seal the deal. I chose to include it in the book so that you will have a better sense of all Tumbling Creek has to offer. Including the named falls, you'll see scene after scene reminiscent of this one: Tumbling Creek is a rugged and steep mountain stream with a seemingly endless supply of cascades and small waterfalls. The cascade featured here is easy to access, and Big Falls is just out of the frame upstream. From this spot, scramble along the creek bank and hillside a few yards to photograph an 8-foot waterfall. Then, continue a delicate scramble along the creek and hillside to take in a few more cascades and slides. Or, make your way back up to the road and walk down about a tenth of a mile or so, and during the months with no leaf cover, you should be able to make out Twin Hollow Falls nestled into the forest across the creek.

You'll have to wade across the stream and venture into the woods about 15 yards or so to photograph Twin Hollow Falls. It's a neat scene, with two separate streams falling over a ledge, converging, and then cascading downstream a few yards before emptying into Tumbling Creek. Due to the proximity, you could possibly visit the falls of Little Stony Creek and Tumbling Creek (page 24) in one day, as they are only about 1.5 hours apart.

Crab Orchard Branch Falls

LOCATION: Guest River Gorge Trail

ADDRESS/GPS FOR THE FALLS: Guest River Gorge Trail Parking Area; 36° 54.77′ N, 82° 26.173′ W

DIRECTIONS: From Coeburn, follow VA-72 South for around 2.5 miles and turn left at the Guest River Gorge Trail sign. Follow for 1.3 miles to the parking area.

WEBSITE: tinyurl.com/guestva

WATERWAY: Crab Orchard Branch

HEIGHT: 15 feet **CREST:** Varies

NEAREST TOWN: Coeburn

HIKE DIFFICULTY: Easy

TRAIL QUALITY: Fine, crushed stone

ROUND-TRIP DISTANCE: 3 miles

ADMISSION: None

TRIP REPORT & TIPS:

From the kiosk at the south end of the parking area, wind your way down to the former railroad grade. Turn right and follow the trail along the scenic Guest River. At around the 0.4-mile mark, pass through the Swede Tunnel, and then, at around the 0.5-mile mark, cross a wooden trestle with great views of the Guest River. At the 1.5-mile mark, you'll reach a small trestle spanning Crab Orchard Branch. In winter and early spring, you'll be able to see the waterfall from the trestle. For a close-up view of the falls, backtrack a short distance to an obvious trail that leads to the waterfall. Near the falls, you might need to bushwhack due to fallen trees. Above the waterfall is private property, so please don't follow the side trail upstream.

Corder Hollow Falls

LOCATION: Jefferson National Forest

ADDRESS/GPS FOR THE FALLS: Devil's Fork Loop Trail / 36° 48.795′ N, 82° 39.462′ W

DIRECTIONS: 0.5 mile from the Devil's Bathtub (page 20)

WEBSITE: None

WATERWAY: Unnamed

HEIGHT: 50 feet **CREST:** Varies

NEAREST TOWN: Dungannon

HIKE DIFFICULTY: Moderate, due to a stream crossing and a very steep descent to the base of the falls

TRAIL QUALITY: Mostly a rocky, root-covered single-track

ROUND-TRIP DISTANCE: 1 mile from Devil's Bathtub and back

ADMISSION: None

TRIP REPORT & TIPS:

While not on a named stream, this waterfall is impressive, and only a half mile away from the Devil's Bathtub. The water comes flying out of Corder Hollow in a narrow chute in a deep forest setting. The trail is high above the stream, so you'll have to make a harrowing descent down to the creek. Look for a section of rope "railing" to aid in the descent and ascent. You'll need to catch this one after a good amount of rainfall, otherwise it's just a trickle.

From the Devil's Bathtub (page 20), follow the trail upstream a short distance and cross the stream. About 0.4 mile from the stream crossing, you'll see the spur trail going steeply down into the canyon to the base of the falls.

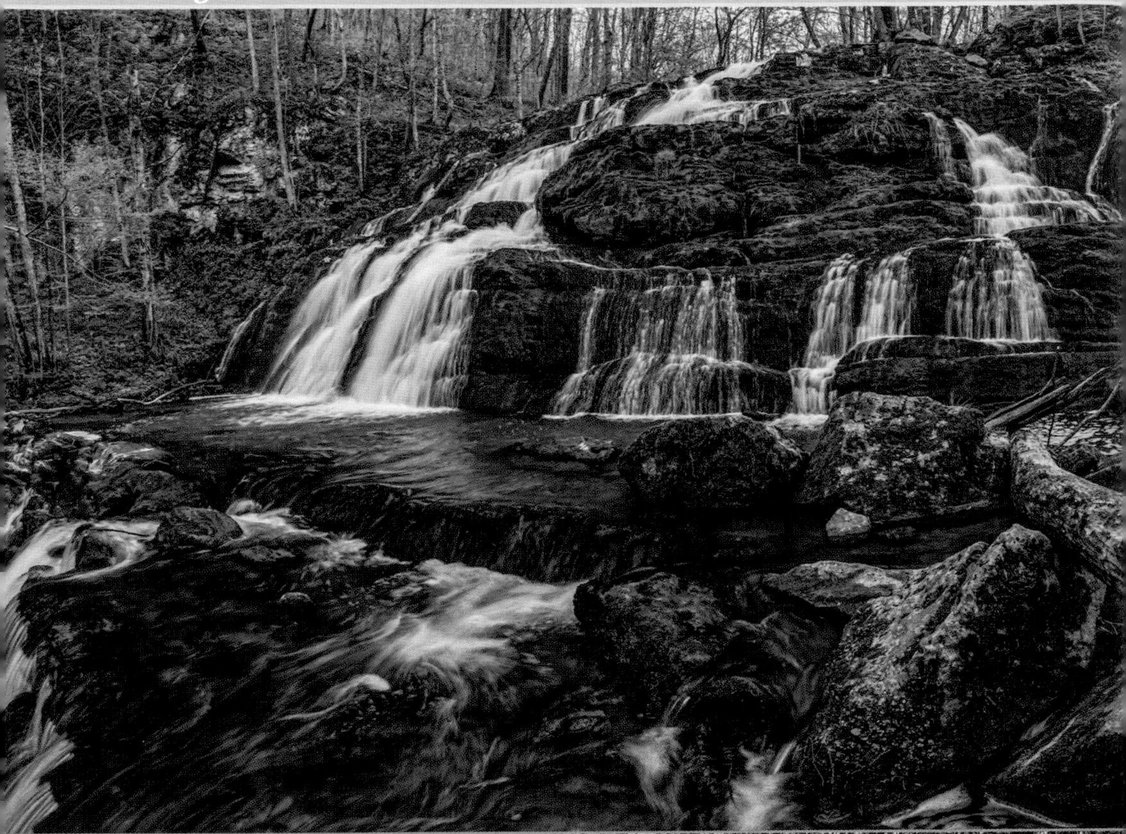

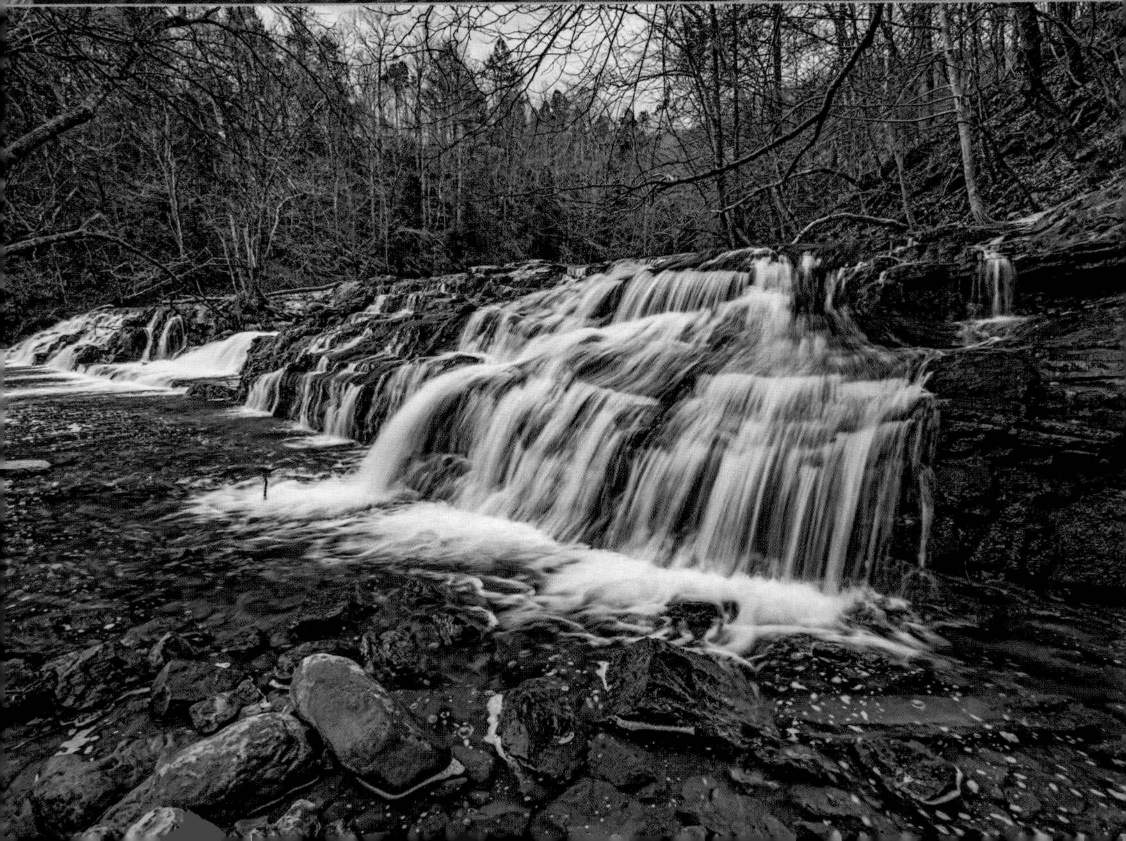

Falls of Logan Creek

LOCATION: Roadside along Route 80

ADDRESS/GPS FOR THE FALLS: Hayters Gap Road; 36° 49.082′N, 81° 55.313′W

DIRECTIONS: From I-81, take the Meadowview exit (exit 24), and follow VA-80 West for 7 miles and look for a pulloff on the right with room for several vehicles. If you cross the bridge over the North Fork Holston River, you've driven about 0.1 mile too far.

WEBSITE: None

WATERWAY: Logan Creek

HEIGHT: 30 feet **CREST:** Varies

NEAREST TOWN: Lindell

HIKE DIFFICULTY: Easy

TRAIL QUALITY: An easy-to-follow dirt path, with a short but steep scramble down to the base of the falls

ROUND-TRIP DISTANCE: 0.2 mile

ADMISSION: None

TRIP REPORT & TIPS:

I stumbled on the Falls of Logan Creek while on Google Earth. There are a couple small falls near the pulloff, and one small waterfall just a few yards downstream of the main falls.

From the parking area, follow the well-worn path downstream for just under a tenth of a mile. There are some possible photo opportunities from up top, but continue following the trail down to the base of the falls. It's pretty tight at the base with little room to maneuver, so bring your wide-angle lens. Just out of frame is a large jumble of fallen trees, so downstream shots won't be too pleasing.

Big Falls

LOCATION: Pinnacle Natural Area Preserve

ADDRESS/GPS FOR THE FALLS: VA-721 near Lebanon, VA; 36° 57.733′N, 82° 3.208′W

DIRECTIONS: From Business US-19/Main Street in Lebanon, follow VA-82 West for a little over a mile. Turn right onto VA-640 and follow for a little over 4 miles, then turn left onto VA-721 and follow to the preserve.

WEBSITE: https://tinyurl.com/pinaccleva

WATERWAY: Big Cedar Creek

HEIGHT: 10 feet **CREST:** Varies

NEAREST TOWN: Lebanon

HIKE DIFFICULTY: Easy with a few relatively steep ascents/descents

TRAIL QUALITY: Good; easy-to-follow gravel road and path

ROUND-TRIP DISTANCE: 2.8 miles if parking in the upper parking lot, 0.6 mile if parking in the lower lot

ADMISSION: None

TRIP REPORT & TIPS:

Big Falls isn't that high, but it's certainly wide. Be sure to spend time taking advantage of all of its different vantage points. If the water level is low enough, you'll be able to drive across Big Cedar Creek on a cement low-water bridge and follow the gravel road to the lower parking area, shaving off all but 0.3 mile of the hike. When I was here, we hiked in from the upper lot, and I'm glad we did, as the bouncy suspension bridge is fun. If you hike down trail a bit from the falls, you'll see "The Pinnacle," a neat rock formation.

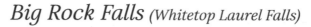

Big Rock Falls *(Whitetop Laurel Falls)*

LOCATION: Virginia Creeper Trail

ADDRESS/GPS FOR THE FALLS: Straight Branch Parking Area; 36° 38.052′ N, 81° 44.936′ W

DIRECTIONS: From Damascus, follow US-58 East, and at the intersection of US-58 and VA-91, continue east on US-58 for about 3 miles. Turn right at the sign for the Straight Branch Parking Area.

WEBSITE: www.vacreepertrail.com

WATERWAY: Whitetop Laurel Creek

HEIGHT: 10 feet **CREST:** Varies

NEAREST TOWN: Damascus

HIKE DIFFICULTY: Easy

TRAIL QUALITY: Crushed gravel on a wide pathway

ROUND-TRIP DISTANCE: 2.1 miles

ADMISSION: None

TRIP REPORT & TIPS:

While not a huge waterfall, Big Rock Falls is in a beautiful setting, and the hike along the Virginia Creeper Trail is equally beautiful. Whitetop Laurel Creek rushed beside us most of the hike and offered many opportunities for photographing stream scenes and moss-laden rocks.

From the Straight Branch Parking Area, turn right and follow the Virginia Creeper Trail downstream. Soon after crossing an old train trestle (the Virginia Creeper Trail is an old railbed), you'll see Big Rock Falls. I scrambled down to a rock ledge first, then dropped on down to the creek bank for more shots. You might be tempted to follow a spur trail before crossing the trestle, but the area is posted, so please don't trespass.

Straight Branch Falls

LOCATION: Roadside along US-58

ADDRESS/GPS FOR THE FALLS: Jeb Stuart Highway/US-58; 36° 38.657′ N, 81° 42.919′ W

DIRECTIONS: From Damascus, follow US-58 East, and at the intersection of US-58 and VA-91, continue east on US-58 for about 4.7 miles. Look for a pullout on the left side of the road just a few yards upstream of the waterfall. There is another pullout on the right just a bit farther up the road.

WEBSITE: None

WATERWAY: Straight Branch

HEIGHT: 20 feet **CREST:** Varies

NEAREST TOWN: Damascus

HIKE DIFFICULTY: Easy, with a little scramble

TRAIL QUALITY: Roadside

ROUND-TRIP DISTANCE: Roadside

ADMISSION: None

TRIP REPORT & TIPS:

You'll notice Straight Branch paralleling Route 58, and you should be able to spot the waterfall from the road. It makes a nice little addition to your trip from shooting Big Rock Falls and on your way to photograph the Chute and other waterfalls in the region.

A simple little hop over the guardrail and a short scramble down to the base of the falls is all you need to do here. This is probably not worth a stop during times of low water flow, but it's definitely worth your time if you find Straight Branch flowing nicely. Just be careful as you walk along the busy roadway.

The Chute

LOCATION: Virginia Creeper Trail

ADDRESS/GPS FOR THE FALLS: Creek Junction Parking Area; 36° 39.016′ N, 81° 40.759′ W

DIRECTIONS: From Damascus, follow US-58 East, and at the intersection of US-58 and VA-91, continue east on US-58 for about 8 more miles, and turn right to the signed Creek Junction Parking Area.

WEBSITE: www.vacreepertrail.com

WATERWAY: Whitetop Laurel Creek

HEIGHT: 10 feet **CREST:** Varies

NEAREST TOWN: Damascus

HIKE DIFFICULTY: Easy

TRAIL QUALITY: Good

ROUND-TRIP DISTANCE: 1.6 miles

ADMISSION: None

TRIP REPORT & TIPS:

While I was along the creek bank at Big Rock Falls my friend Kevin struck up a conversation with another hiker. In it, he learned about the Chute, which was just as our new friend described it. The canyon narrows and the wide, placid waters of Whitetop Laurel Creek are pinched tight and flow through cascades and slides.

From the parking area, don't climb up to the Virginia Creeper Trail, but hike the creek-side angler's trail to its junction with the Virginia Creeper Trail about a mile downstream. Continue on the Virginia Creeper Trail, and shortly after crossing a trestle, the creek begins to narrow and make its way through the Chute. Several spur trails lead you to vantages of various slides, cascades, and waterfalls.

Cabin Creek Cascade

LOCATION: Grayson Highlands State Park

ADDRESS/GPS FOR THE FALLS: Massie Gap Parking Area; 36° 37.902′ N, 81° 31.102′ W

DIRECTIONS: The Massie Gap parking area is 3.5 miles from the park entrance, and the Cabin Creek trailhead is in the middle of the parking area.

WEBSITE: tinyurl.com/graysonva

WATERWAY: Cabin Creek

HEIGHT: 8 feet **CREST:** Varies

NEAREST TOWN: Volney

HIKE DIFFICULTY: Moderate

TRAIL QUALITY: Rocky, with exposed roots and a few stream crossings on a very small unnamed creek

ROUND-TRIP DISTANCE: The Cabin Creek Trail is a 1.9-mile lollipop loop

ADMISSION: Parking fee is $5 for VA residents and $7 for nonresidents

TRIP REPORT & TIPS:

I'd heard Cabin Creek had only two falls, so I was excited to visit with my friend Kevin and learn there are at least four waterfalls along the Cabin Creek Trail.

From the trailhead, follow the yellow-blazed trail and begin a steady descent through a rhododendron tunnel. At 0.2 mile you'll cross a horse trail and then see a trail register. The loop section begins at 0.3 mile; bear to the left and continue downhill. At the 0.8-mile mark, you'll see Cabin Creek a short distance below the trail. Follow a spur trail down to this beautiful cascade.

Lower Cabin Creek Falls

LOCATION: Grayson Highlands State Park

ADDRESS/GPS FOR THE FALLS: Massie Gap Parking Area; 36° 38.017′ N, 81° 31.155′ W

DIRECTIONS: The Massie Gap parking area is 3.5 miles from the park entrance, and the Cabin Creek trailhead is in the middle of the parking area.

WEBSITE: tinyurl.com/graysonva

WATERWAY: Cabin Creek

HEIGHT: 30 feet **CREST:** Varies

NEAREST TOWN: Volney

HIKE DIFFICULTY: Moderate

TRAIL QUALITY: Rocky, with exposed roots and a few stream crossings on a very small unnamed creek

ROUND-TRIP DISTANCE: The Cabin Creek Trail is a 1.9-mile lollipop loop

ADMISSION: Parking fee is $5 for VA residents, and $7 for nonresidents

TRIP REPORT & TIPS:

From the trailhead, follow the yellow-blazed trail and begin a steady descent through a rhododendron tunnel. The loop section begins at 0.3 mile; bear to the left and continue downhill. At the 0.8-mile mark you'll see the Cabin Creek Cascade featured on page 38. Continue following the trail upstream for about 300 yards to the Lower Falls.

The Lower Falls is a beauty nestled in a cove-like area surrounded by lush greens and large boulders. Cabin Creek flows over the ledge in three distinct courses into a shallow pool, creating an impressive scene. There are many vantage points here, so spend some time exploring.

Middle Cabin Creek Falls

LOCATION: Grayson Highlands State Park

ADDRESS/GPS FOR THE FALLS: Massie Gap Parking Area; 36° 38.035′ N, 81° 31.172′ W

DIRECTIONS: The Massie Gap parking area is 3.5 miles from the park entrance, and the Cabin Creek trailhead is in the middle of the parking area.

WEBSITE: tinyurl.com/graysonva

WATERWAY: Cabin Creek

HEIGHT: 15 feet **CREST:** Varies

NEAREST TOWN: Volney

HIKE DIFFICULTY: Moderate

TRAIL QUALITY: Rocky, with exposed roots and a few stream crossings on a very small unnamed creek

ROUND-TRIP DISTANCE: The Cabin Creek Trail is a 1.9-mile lollipop loop

ADMISSION: Parking fee is $5 for VA residents, and $7 for nonresidents

TRIP REPORT & TIPS:

From the trailhead, follow the yellow-blazed trail and begin a steady descent through a rhododendron tunnel. The loop section begins at 0.3 mile, bear to the left and continue downhill. At the 0.8-mile mark you'll see the Cabin Creek Cascade featured on page 38, and in 300 yards you'll reach the Lower Falls featured above. Continue on the trail for about 50 yards to the Middle Falls. Carefully work your way down a short bank and hop across a couple small boulders to access the falls. This waterfall is neat because at the top the water is spread out on a wide ledge, but near the bottom it is squeezed into a narrow chute.

Upper Cabin Creek Falls

LOCATION: Grayson Highlands State Park

ADDRESS/GPS FOR THE FALLS: Massie Gap Parking Area; 36° 38.281′N, 81° 31.255′W

DIRECTIONS: The Massie Gap parking area is 3.5 miles from the park entrance, and the Cabin Creek trailhead is in the middle of the parking area.

WEBSITE: tinyurl.com/graysonva

WATERWAY: Cabin Creek

HEIGHT: 20 feet **CREST:** Varies

NEAREST TOWN: Volney

HIKE DIFFICULTY: Moderate

TRAIL QUALITY: Rocky, with exposed roots and a few stream crossings on a tiny unnamed creek

ROUND-TRIP DISTANCE: The Cabin Creek Trail is a 1.9-mile lollipop loop

ADMISSION: Parking fee is $5 for VA residents, and $7 for nonresidents

TRIP REPORT & TIPS:

From the trailhead, follow the yellow-blazed trail and begin a steady descent through a rhododendron tunnel. The loop section begins at 0.3 mile; bear to the left and continue downhill, passing the Cabin Creek Cascade and the Lower and Middle Cabin Creek Falls along the way. At about the 1.45-mile mark, you'll reach a trail junction and sign. Here, the Cabin Creek Trail makes a sharp right, but stay straight along a rather steep and rocky spur trail for about 70 yards to the Upper Falls. Overall, Cabin Creek didn't disappoint.

To get back to the Cabin Creek Trail, simply retrace your steps to the trail junction and sign. Bear left and follow the trail as it gently leads uphill, completing the loop.

Wilson Creek Falls

LOCATION: Grayson Highlands State Park

ADDRESS/GPS FOR THE FALLS: Parking and trailhead is directly across the road from the General Store; 36° 38.761′N, 81° 29.37′W

DIRECTIONS: From the park's entrance, drive 3.2 miles, then turn right at the sign for the campground. Follow for 1.2 miles to the General Store.

WEBSITE: tinyurl.com/graysonva

WATERWAY: Wilson Creek

HEIGHT: 25 feet **CREST:** Varies

NEAREST TOWN: Volney

HIKE DIFFICULTY: Moderate

TRAIL QUALITY: Rocky, with exposed roots

ROUND-TRIP DISTANCE: 1.6 miles

ADMISSION: Parking fee is $5 for VA residents, and $7 for nonresidents

TRIP REPORT & TIPS:

This short hike descends steeply from the trailhead, which is located in the parking area directly across from the General Store. Hike 0.5 mile to the creek and a triangle shelter. From the shelter, continue following the red-blazed Wilson Creek Trail through a rhododendron tunnel for 0.3 mile to the falls. Kevin and I were fortunate to visit here just after a rain shower, and I think it's best for you to do the same if possible. As you can see, this waterfall is essentially a series of ledges, and when the exposed sections are wet, the photos really pop. I loved the setting here— the creek is lined with rhododendron, and the trail deposits you on a massive boulder just above the falls.

Fox Creek Falls

LOCATION: Roadside near Troutdale

ADDRESS/GPS FOR THE FALLS: County Road 603; 36° 41.823′ N, 81° 27.989′ W

DIRECTIONS: From the entrance to Grayson Highlands State Park, follow US-58 East for 7.7 miles. Turn left onto VA-16 North and follow for 7 miles. Turn left onto VA-603 and follow for 1.7 miles. A pullout with room for 3 vehicles is on the right.

WEBSITE: None

WATERWAY: Fox Creek

HEIGHT: 10 feet **CREST:** Varies

NEAREST TOWN: Troutdale

HIKE DIFFICULTY: Short but steep scramble down to the falls

TRAIL QUALITY: Narrow dirt path

ROUND-TRIP DISTANCE: 50 yards

ADMISSION: None

TRIP REPORT & TIPS:

From the pullout on VA-603, you'll notice a couple paths leading down to the creek. Take the steep one near the upper portion of the pullout and follow about 25 yards down to the stream.

Fox Creek and Comers Creek (below) are two perfect streams to add to your visit to Grayson Highlands State Park. They're probably not a destination all to themselves but certainly worth your time if you're in the area. The setting here is beautiful, with Fox Creek cascading over massive bedrock surrounded by moss-covered rocks and small boulders.

Comers Creek Falls

LOCATION: Jefferson National Forest

ADDRESS/GPS FOR THE FALLS: VA-741; 36° 42.849′ N, 81° 28.448′ W

DIRECTIONS: Since Fox Creek Falls and Comers Creek Falls are less than 4 miles apart, I'm routing you to Comers Creek from Fox Creek. From Fox Creek Falls, drive back 1.7 miles on VA-603, and turn left onto VA-16 North. Follow for 1.7 miles, and turn left onto VA-741 and follow for about 0.3 mile to a pulloff on the left.

WEBSITE: None

WATERWAY: Comers Creek

HEIGHT: 15 feet **CREST:** Varies

NEAREST TOWN: Volney

HIKE DIFFICULTY: Easy

TRAIL QUALITY: Dirt path

ROUND-TRIP DISTANCE: 0.7 mile

ADMISSION: None

TRIP REPORT & TIPS:

From the pullout, follow the sign for the blue-blazed Comers Creek Trail. At the 0.2-mile mark you'll reach a junction with the yellow-blazed Iron Mountain Trail; stay on Comer's Creek Trail. At the 0.3-mile mark, make a sharp right onto the white-blazed Appalachian Trail, and follow for another 0.1 mile to a footbridge and the waterfall.

Comers Creek Falls is a little beauty just off the famed Appalachian Trail. Bring your extreme wide-angle lens to this one. There are a couple fallen trees near the base of the falls; I had to shoot wide to keep the trees from marring the view.

More Virginia Falls

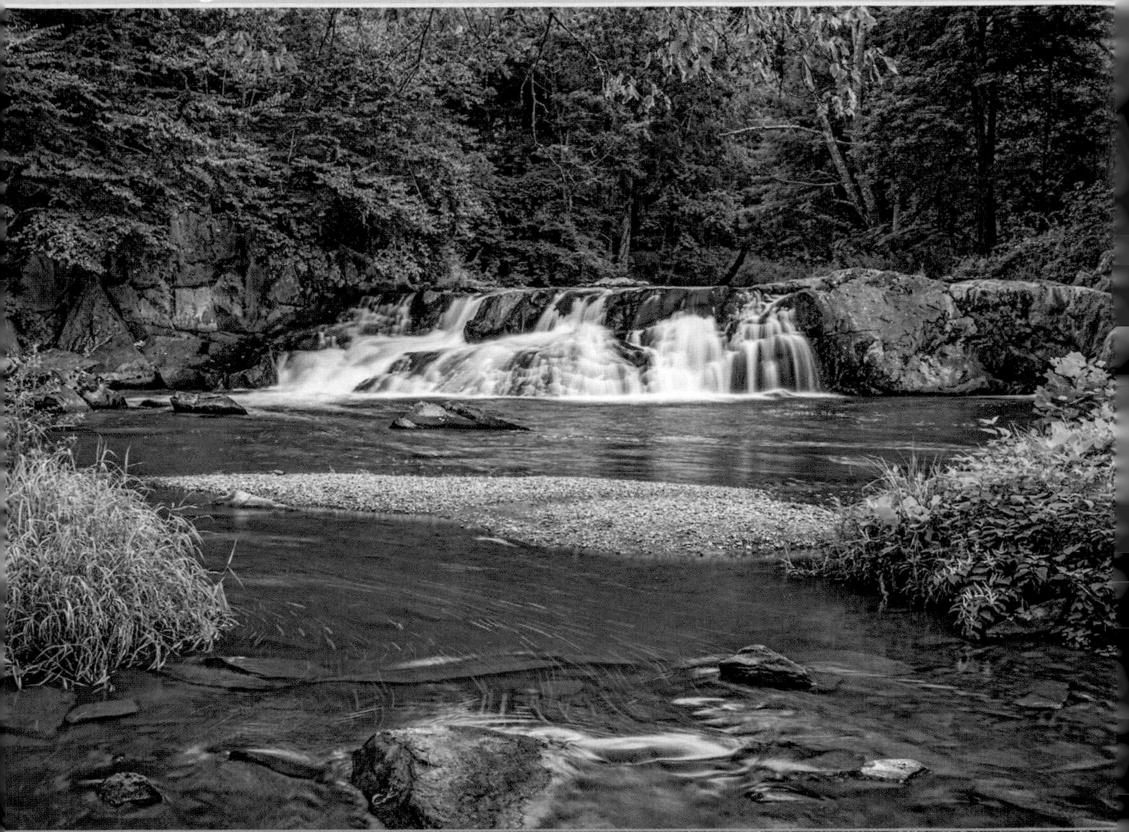

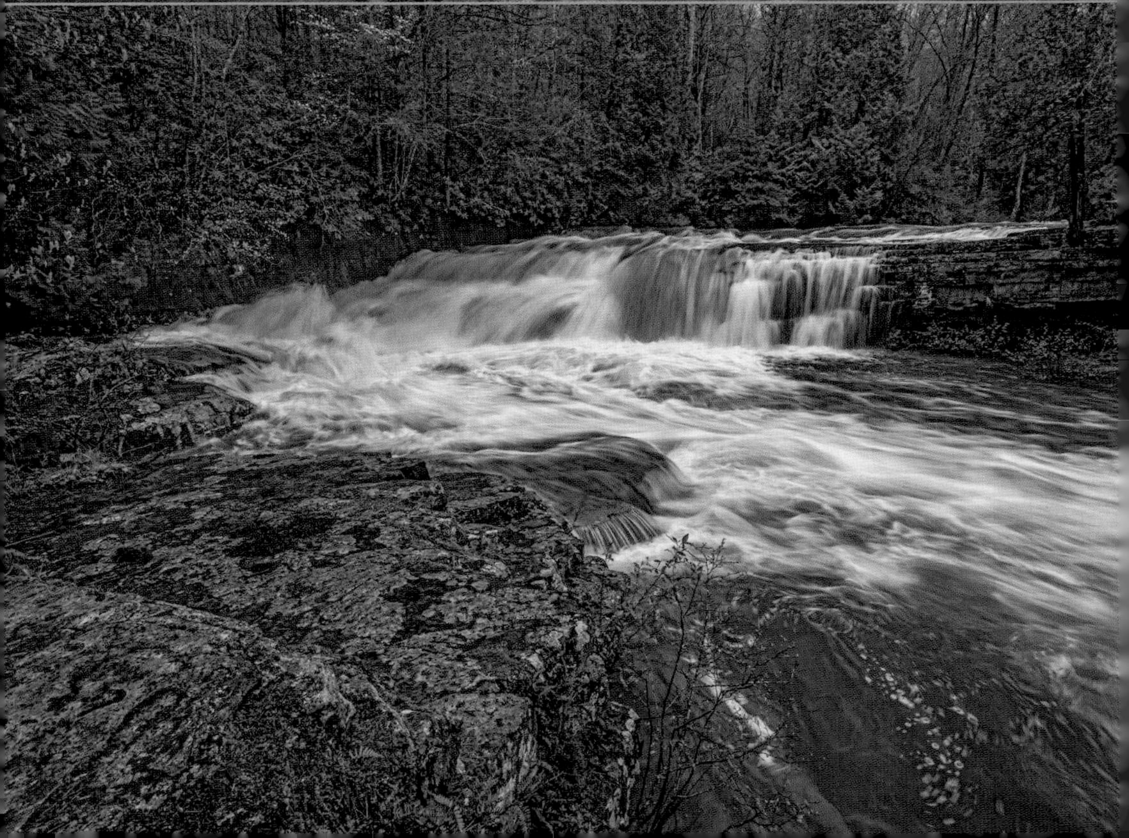

Chestnut Creek Falls

LOCATION: New River Trail State Park

ADDRESS/GPS FOR THE FALLS: Chestnut Yard Parking Area; 36° 42.944′N, 80° 54.551′W

DIRECTIONS: From US-58/US-221 in Galax, turn north onto Glendale Road (near the Subway Restaurant), follow for 0.6 mile to a left turn onto VA-721 (Cliffview Road), and then follow for 2 miles. Turn right onto VA-607 for 2.8 miles to the parking area on the right.

WEBSITE: None

WATERWAY: Chestnut Creek

HEIGHT: 8 feet **CREST:** Varies

NEAREST TOWN: Galax

HIKE DIFFICULTY: Easy

TRAIL QUALITY: The rail-trail is composed of fine, crushed stone

ROUND-TRIP DISTANCE: 1.9 miles

ADMISSION: $5 parking fee

TRIP REPORT & TIPS:

At the parking area, hike upstream on the New River Trail for just under 1 mile to an old railroad trestle and a picnic shelter. From the picnic shelter, simply walk down through the grass field to the creek and have a ball shooting this little beauty. I loved the setting here, as there are numerous vantage points to shoot from, and the easy hike was quite welcome on a warm summer day.

Falls of Dismal

LOCATION: Jefferson National Forest

ADDRESS/GPS FOR THE FALLS: Dismal Creek Road; 37° 11.154′N, 80° 54.102′W

DIRECTIONS: From the Bland, VA, exit (exit 52), take US-52 east into Bland, then follow VA-42 East for 13.2 miles. Turn left onto VA-606 and follow for 1 mile, then turn right onto Forest Road 201 (Dismal Creek Road). Follow for 1 mile to parking on the right.

WEBSITE: tinyurl.com/dismalva

WATERWAY: Dismal Creek

HEIGHT: 15 feet **CREST:** Varies

NEAREST TOWN: Bland

HIKE DIFFICULTY: Easy

TRAIL QUALITY: Good

ROUND-TRIP DISTANCE: 100 yards

ADMISSION: None

TRIP REPORT & TIPS:

Located in a picturesque setting, Dismal Creek flows toward a stair-step ledge, angles toward the right side of the stream against a sheer rock face, and then falls into a large pool. There are a couple vantage points near the trail that will allow you to feature the forest and Dismal Creek in the background. Downstream shots with the cascading stream as the foreground are also pleasing. It's a beautiful little waterfall and accessible with very little effort. From the roadside parking, simply follow the path about 50 yards down to the stream. If you happen to be hiking the Appalachian Trail, there is a spur trail leading down to the waterfall from the opposite side of the creek.

The Cascades

The Cascades is one of the prettiest waterfalls in the two Virginias, and a Must-Do hike.

Little Stony Creek

The Cascades

The Cascades National Recreation Trail is one of the most beautiful waterfall and creek hikes in Virginia.

LOCATION: Jefferson National Forest

ADDRESS/GPS FOR THE FALLS: Cascades National Recreation Trail; 37° 22.07' N, 80° 34.52' W

DIRECTIONS: From Pembroke, follow VA-623/Cascade Drive 3.5 miles to the parking area.

WEBSITE: tinyurl.com/cascadesva

WATERWAY: Little Stony Creek

HEIGHT: 66 feet **CREST:** Varies

NEAREST TOWN: Pembroke

HIKE DIFFICULTY: Easy, with several moderate ascents and descents

TRAIL QUALITY: Good, with some sections with rocks and roots

ROUND-TRIP DISTANCE: 4 miles

ADMISSION: $3 per vehicle; the parking area is open sunrise to sunset

TRIP REPORT & TIPS:

The Cascades is one of the first waterfalls I can recall seeing. As a young teen on a trip to visit my grandparents' place in nearby West Virginia, my Aunt Sue gathered up a few of my cousins and me for a hike here. I've been back numerous times since then, and on my most recent visit, I met my friend Kevin there. We had both hiked it about nine years previous to the day, and it was good to hike to the falls with him again.

If you're like me, you'll spend more time photographing the many stream scenes along the hike than photographing the main feature. It is such an incredible creek, with cascade after cascade; you'll find it is especially beautiful with the new greenery of spring and during fall foliage season.

You can make your way up to the Cascades via two routes. The upper trail is an old fire road and is pretty much uphill all the way, with few views of Little Stony Creek. I always save the upper trail for the trip back to the parking area, since it's more of a direct route and downhill all the way. The lower trail is a gem, offering countless opportunities to take in the scenic stream and all of the cascades and small waterfalls. You'll hear the roar of the Cascades before you see them, and at about 0.1 mile from the falls, you'll catch your first glimpse of this Virginia classic. There are a couple viewing platforms and several vantage points near the trail, but I always like hopping in the creek and shooting from various positions there. To access the upper trail for your trek back down to the parking area, climb some steps and follow the path up to the upper trail. If you want to return to the parking area, go left. For another great waterfall featured on page 52, go right.

The Upper Cascades

This hidden beauty is only a half mile away from the Cascades.

The Upper Cascades

The Upper Cascades

You're so close, don't miss this one!

LOCATION: Jefferson National Forest

ADDRESS/GPS FOR THE FALLS: Upper Falls Spur Trail; 37° 22.344′ N, 80° 34.465′ W

DIRECTIONS: From Pembroke, follow VA-623/Cascade Drive 3.5 miles to the parking area.

WEBSITE: tinyurl.com/cascadesva

WATERWAY: Little Stony Creek

HEIGHT: 20 feet **CREST:** Varies

NEAREST TOWN: Pembroke

HIKE DIFFICULTY: Moderate, due to a rocky ascent and descent

TRAIL QUALITY: Fair, with soggy, rock-strewn sections

ROUND-TRIP DISTANCE: 5 miles from the Cascades parking area and back

ADMISSION: $3 per vehicle

TRIP REPORT & TIPS:

In the previous listing, I mentioned a visit that I made with my friend Kevin about nine years prior to our most recent trip to the Cascades. The ultimate goal of that visit was to find the Upper Falls; there were very few mentions or photos of it at that time. Kevin had his son Austin with him, so we took some time for the obligatory portraits of ourselves in front of the Cascades, and then we made our way to the upper trail and to the Upper Cascades. Due to how late it was (the parking area closes at sunset), I only had time to fire off a couple frames before we had to hustle back down the trail to our vehicles.

Fast forward nine years, and Kevin and I are back at the Upper Cascades with plenty of time to spare. The spur trail deposits you at the ledge of the falls, with an obvious path to the right through the rhododendron thickets down to the creek. I was eager to scramble down and work on all the compositions I was unable to make nine years prior, and Kevin was itching to explore a path across the creek that led through the woods.

As it turned out, the Upper Cascades is my kind of waterfall. Boasting multiple ledges, the waters of Little Stony Creek cascade this way and that for about 20 feet before entering the large pool area below the falls. The creek bank is choked with rhododendron, and there's not as much room to maneuver as I'd like, so I did what any self-respecting waterfall photographer would do and hopped into the creek, photographing from both sides of the stream. I'm thankful that we had plenty of time that day, as the heavy cover started to wane and I had to patiently wait for an occasional dark cloud to obscure the sun.

From the parking area, follow the lower trail for 2 miles to the Cascades (page 48). Take the steps up from the falls and follow the path to its intersection with the upper trail. Go right and follow uphill, and at around 0.4 mile, the trail bears left to continue up to Barney's Wall, but you will see a spur trail to the right leading down to the creek through a rhododendron tunnel. Follow the spur trail about 0.1 mile to the ledge of the Upper Falls.

While a trip to the Cascades (page 48) should be on your must-do list, so should a short additional trip to the Upper Cascades. I'm already looking forward to my next visit, and I can promise you it won't take me nine years to get back there.

Falling Spring Falls

"The only remarkable Cascade in this country is that of the Falling Spring in Augusta." ~Thomas Jefferson

Falling Spring Falls

The waters of Falling Spring are fed by several underground springs, with water both warm and cold, that combine to make the average water temperature here around 65 degrees.

LOCATION: Just off of US-220 near Covington

ADDRESS/GPS FOR THE FALLS: US-220/Hot Springs Road; 37° 52.056′ N, 79° 56.87′ W

DIRECTIONS: From I-64 in Covington, take exit 16 to US-220 North and follow for about 10 miles. The falls and parking area are on the left.

WEBSITE: tinyurl.com/fallingspringva

WATERWAY: Falling Spring

HEIGHT: 80 feet **CREST:** Varies

NEAREST TOWN: Covington

HIKE DIFFICULTY: Roadside View

TRAIL QUALITY: Roadside View

ROUND-TRIP DISTANCE: Roadside View

ADMISSION: None

TRIP REPORT & TIPS:

Thomas Jefferson was right: Falling Spring Falls is quite remarkable! Emerging seemingly out of nowhere amid a thick forest, the waters of Falling Spring leap 80 feet to a sculpted travertine base. The travertine is deposited by the limestone waters that are fed by several underground springs nearby. Jefferson also made a couple of questionable statements. One was that Falling Spring Falls was "the only remarkable cascade in this country (region or area)." I'm just going to assume he had yet to visit the Cascades, Crabtree Falls, and other equally remarkable waterfalls in Virginia. Another statement was that "it falls over a rock 200 feet into the valley below." While it is an impressive drop, it is nowhere near 200 feet, leading many to wonder how he got it so wrong. Some theories are that the buildup of travertine over the years has perhaps shortened the length of the drop. But there are reports that the stream was actually rerouted many years ago due to mining efforts, so the location of the waterfall you see today may not be where Jefferson saw it.

With all that said, Falling Spring Falls is indeed remarkable and certainly worthy of the short drive from I-64 in Covington. It is one of the few Virginia waterfalls I visited prior to this book project, and I've never been disappointed here. It's one of those rare waterfalls that look awesome on a sunny day once the sun is in proper position. Due to the expansive view beyond the falls, including a brilliant blue sky really works wonders here. It's also great to go wide here when the sky is full of epic light and cloud cover, or even just some neat, moody clouds. You won't have tons of vantage points available to you from the viewing area, but you'll have no trouble making fantastic images here; the setting is that good. I've seen some spectacular images from the base of the falls, but technically, it is illegal to follow an unofficial path down to the base. There is a fence blocking the way, and signs warning of possible citations and fines if you are caught, so keep that in mind.

If you're a covered bridge fan, the unique Humpback Covered Bridge is about 5 miles from Covington via I-64 West.

Stiles Falls

LOCATION: Alta Mons Summer Camp

ADDRESS/GPS FOR THE FALLS: 2842 Crockett Springs Road, Shawsville, VA 24162; 37° 4.895′ N, 80° 15.963′ W

DIRECTIONS: From Christiansburg, take the I-81 Shawsville/Elliston exit (exit 118C if northbound, 118B if southbound), and head east on US-11/US-460 for about 6 miles to Shawsville. Turn right onto VA-637/Alleghany Spring Road. Follow for 6 miles, and turn right onto Crockett Springs Road, and follow to the parking area.

WEBSITE: www.altamons.org/hiking.html

WATERWAY: Purgatory Creek

HEIGHT: 40 feet **CREST:** Varies

NEAREST TOWN: Shawsville

HIKE DIFFICULTY: Easy to the first creek crossing, then moderate due to a few ascents/descents and additional creek crossings

TRAIL QUALITY: Well-marked and easy-to-follow gravel road to the first stream crossing, then a wide and rocky dirt path

ROUND-TRIP DISTANCE: About 3 miles

ADMISSION: None, but donations are accepted and appreciated

TRIP REPORT & TIPS:

Alta Mons is a summer camp and retreat center owned by the Roanoke District of the United Methodist Church. It is home to Stiles Falls, an awe-inspiring waterfall, and the rugged, boulder-strewn setting is simply fantastic. They graciously allow public access to their property, so please treat it with respect. The property closes at 5:00 pm, so arrive early in the day so that you'll have plenty of time to photograph Stiles Falls. Lastly, be sure to check their website before visiting. They do close the property for retreats and summer camp, so it's best to confirm they'll be open on your visit.

For about a mile, your walk from the parking area will be a gentle stroll through the Alta Mons campus. Following the white blazes, you'll leave the gravel road and parallel the stream a short distance to the first stream crossing. This is where you leave the campus area and venture into the woods for about 0.5 mile. The trail is easy to follow, and after the next stream crossing, you'll begin to reach the first of a few ascents and descents. Cross the stream a final time, and after one more ascent, you'll catch your first glimpse of Stiles Falls.

Roaring Run Falls

LOCATION: Jefferson National Forest

ADDRESS/GPS FOR THE FALLS: Roaring Run Road; 37° 42.607' N, 79° 53.999' W

DIRECTIONS: From Fincastle, follow US-220 North for a little over 12 miles, then turn left onto VA-615 and follow for 5.5 miles to a right turn onto VA-621. Follow for 0.9 mile, and turn left into the Roaring Run-Day Use Area.

WEBSITE: tinyurl.com/roaringrunva

WATERWAY: Roaring Run

HEIGHT: 40 feet **CREST:** Varies

NEAREST TOWN: Eagle Rock

HIKE DIFFICULTY: An easy, straight forward out-and-back

TRAIL QUALITY: Hard packed dirt path with wooden foot bridges at the stream crossings; some stone steps aid your ascent near the end of the trail.

ROUND-TRIP DISTANCE: 1.3 miles

ADMISSION: None

TRIP REPORT & TIPS:

The beautiful scenery along the way to Roaring Run Falls makes this another great Virginia waterfall hike. The relatively easy trail and short walk also make for a good family outing. My friend Kevin and I visited here for the first time in late winter, and I made a return visit in the late summer. As we walked up the trail, we were met with numerous cascades, small waterfalls, and natural waterslides. Once we reached Roaring Run Falls, I had a difficult time deciding where to start shooting first, as there were so many vantage points to choose from. The rocks are very slippery here, and we couldn't help but notice several signs warning us to stay off of them. Apparently, a few folks have not heeded those signs and fell to their deaths, so please be careful.

The trail starts just beyond the parking area at a kiosk to the left of the restrooms. Follow along Roaring Run, passing numerous photo opportunities along the way. Near the falls, you'll have to ascend a few steps, but they're not at all difficult. Be sure to check out the iron furnace on-site near the parking area. It dates back to before the Civil War and has a couple signs with information regarding its use and history. See page 65 for additional waterfall options on the trail.

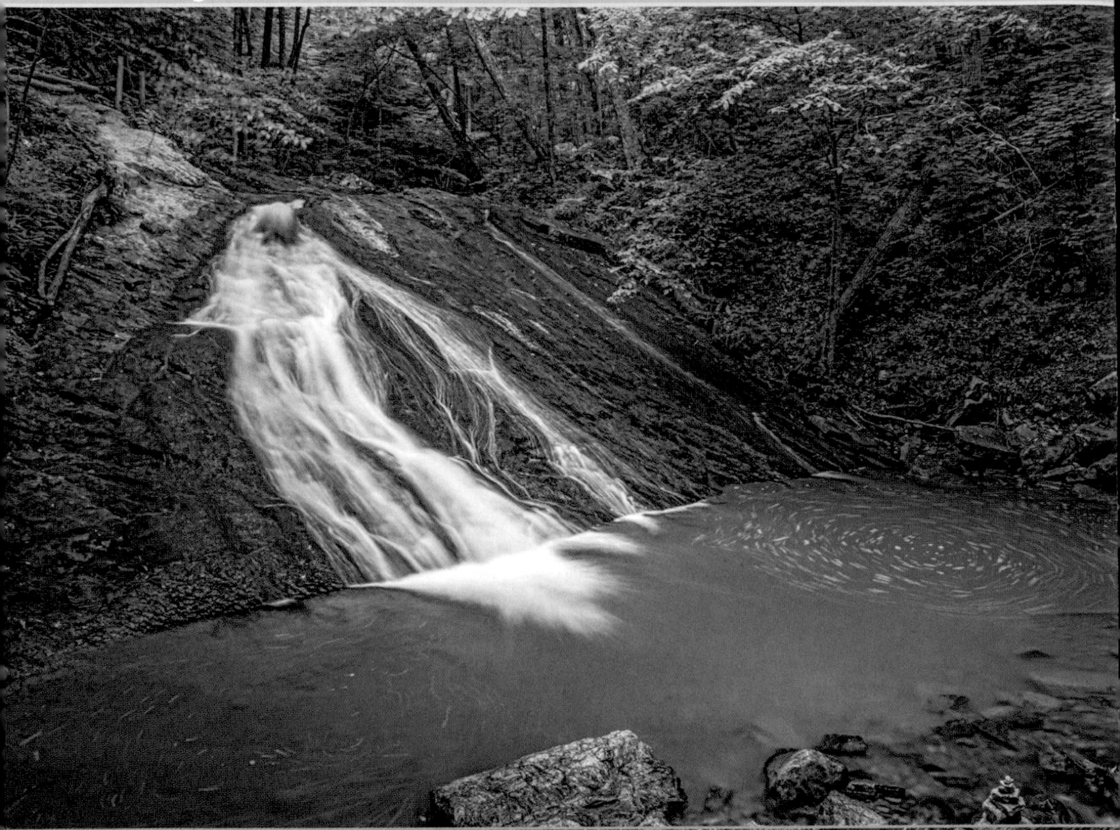

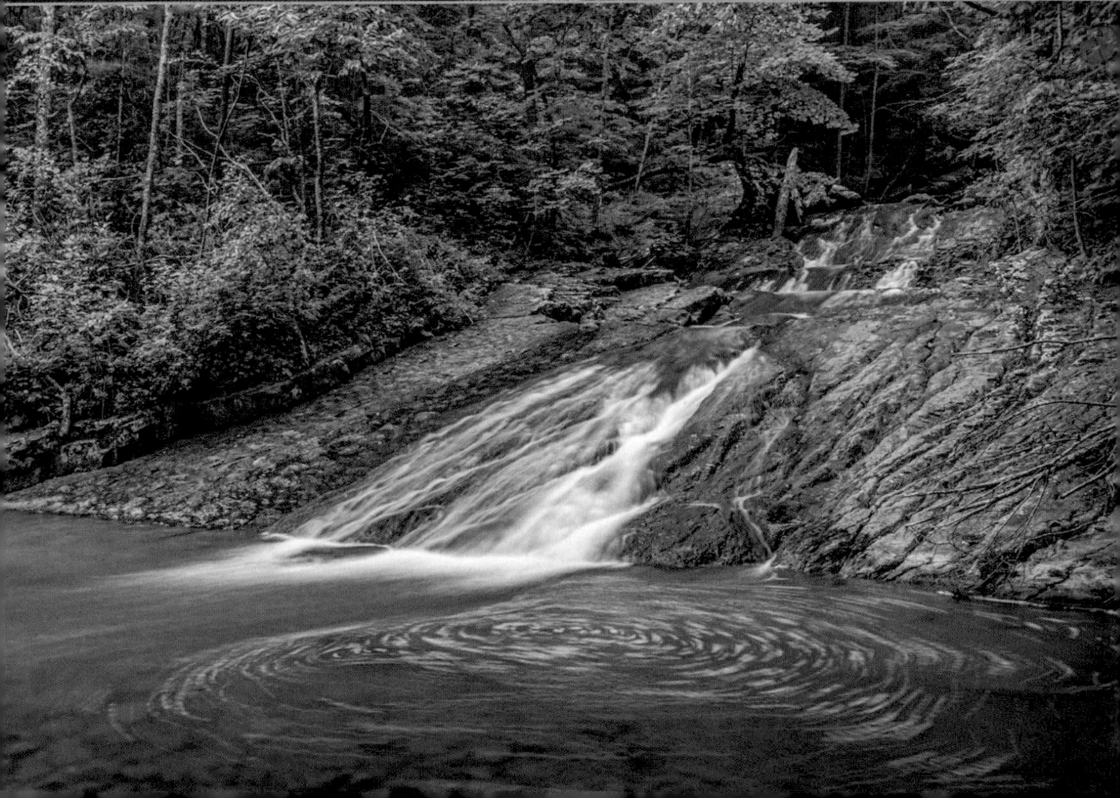

Roaring Run Slide

LOCATION: Jefferson National Forest

ADDRESS/GPS FOR THE FALLS: Roaring Run Road; 37° 42.624' N, 79° 53.77' W

DIRECTIONS: From Fincastle, follow US-220 North for a little over 12 miles, then turn left onto VA-615 and follow for 5.5 miles to a right turn onto VA-621. Follow for 0.9 mile, and turn left into the Roaring Run Day-Use Area.

WEBSITE: tinyurl.com/roaringrunva

WATERWAY: Roaring Run

HEIGHT: 25 feet **CREST:** Varies

NEAREST TOWN: Eagle Rock

HIKE DIFFICULTY: Easy

TRAIL QUALITY: Hard-packed dirt path

ROUND-TRIP DISTANCE: 0.5 mile from trailhead and back

ADMISSION: None

TRIP REPORT & TIPS:

On my first visit to Roaring Run on a late-winter day, I was in a hurry to photograph the big waterfall and move on to more waterfalls in the region. I found myself here again during late summer, and I made time to photograph this beautiful slide. It was easy for me to imagine the fun that folks have sliding down into the deep pool below, and I hope to bring my wife and daughter here to do just that in a few years, when Hannah is a little older and can safely navigate the slide.

From the trailhead, you'll reach this sliding beauty at the 0.25-mile mark. Continue following the trail upstream for the next listing, and, ultimately, Roaring Run Falls featured on page 62.

Double Falls on Roaring Run

LOCATION: Jefferson National Forest

ADDRESS/GPS FOR THE FALLS: Roaring Run Road; 37° 42.666' N, 79° 53.92' W

DIRECTIONS: From Fincastle, follow US-220 North for a little over 12 miles, then turn left onto VA-615 and follow for 5.5 miles to a right turn onto VA-621. Follow for 0.9 mile, and turn left into the Roaring Run Day-Use Area.

WEBSITE: tinyurl.com/roaringrunva

WATERWAY: Roaring Run

HEIGHT: A double drop of about 35 feet in all

CREST: Varies

NEAREST TOWN: Eagle Rock

HIKE DIFFICULTY: Easy

TRAIL QUALITY: Hard-packed dirt path

ROUND-TRIP DISTANCE: 0.8 mile from trailhead and back

ADMISSION: None

TRIP REPORT & TIPS:

From the Roaring Run Slide, continue on the trail for about 0.2 mile; just before a set of stone steps leading up to Roaring Run Falls, you'll reach the Double Falls. The main attraction, Roaring Run Falls, is just 0.3 mile upstream from this point.

I'm glad that I made it back here to photograph this waterfall and the slide, downstream. There is so much beauty packed into a short distance here; definitely add this to your list of waterfall excursions.

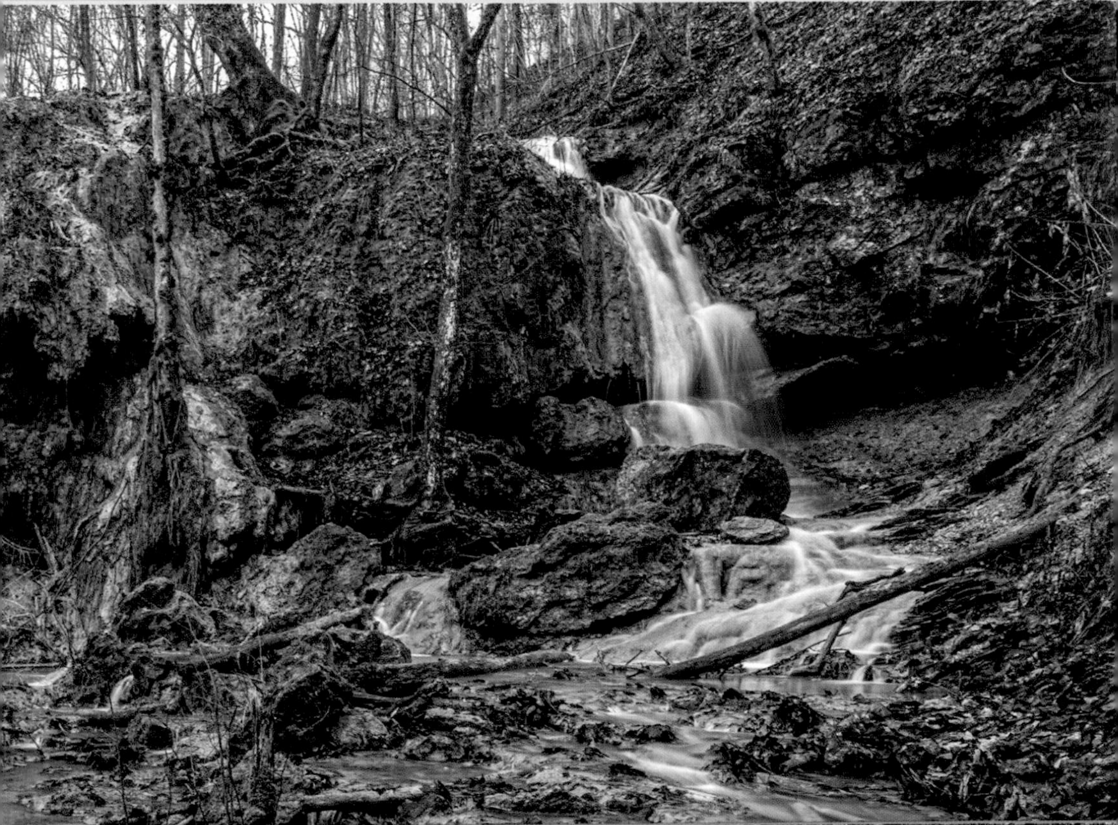

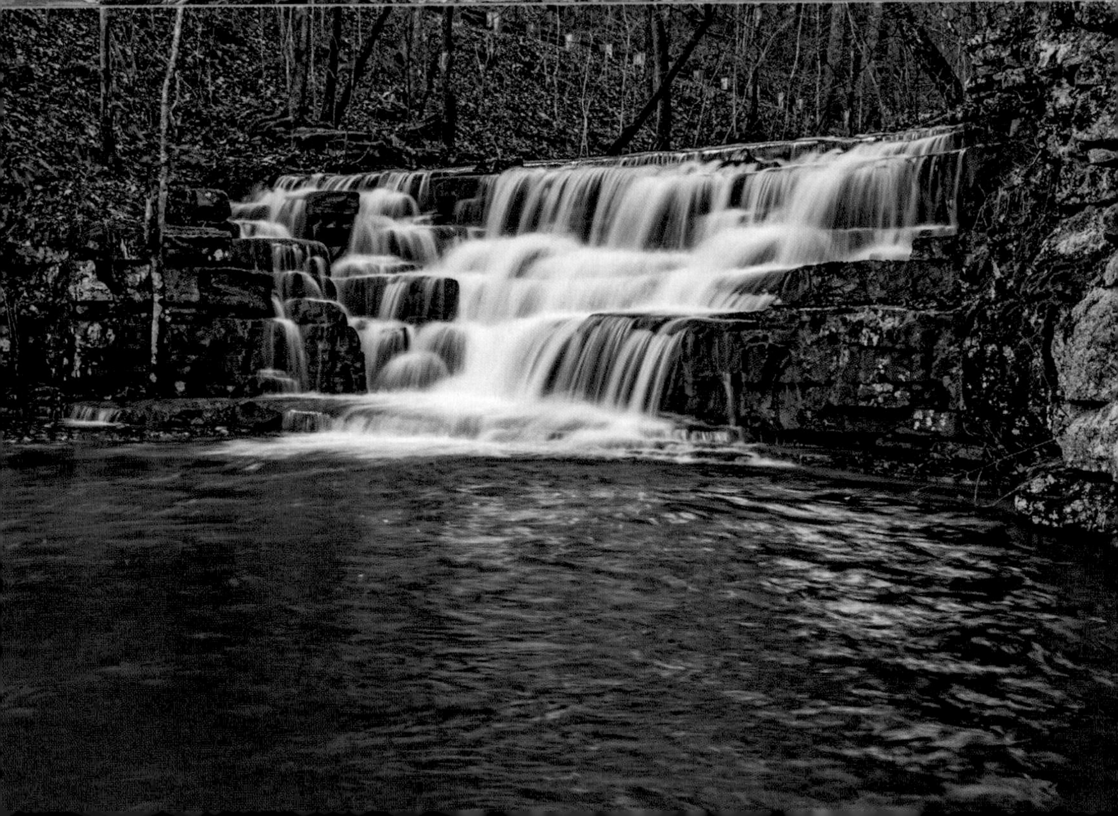

Waterfall at Falls Ridge

LOCATION: Falls Ridge Preserve

ADDRESS/GPS FOR THE FALLS: Falls Ridge Road; 37° 11.378′ N, 80° 19.19′ W

DIRECTIONS: From I-81, southwest of Roanoke, take the Ironto/VA-603 exit (exit 128); this exit is about 9 miles south of Salem and 10 miles north of Christiansburg. Follow VA-603/North Fork Road for 7 miles, and look for a red private bridge and Falls Ridge Road on the left. Turn left onto Falls Ridge Road and cross the bridge, then almost immediately cross a set of railroad tracks. Take a left onto a gravel road after crossing the tracks, and follow for about 0.3 mile and bear left and into the Nature Conservancy parking area at the fork.

WEBSITE: tinyurl.com/fallsridgeva

WATERWAY: Spring fed

HEIGHT: 70 feet **CREST:** Varies

NEAREST TOWN: Elliston

HIKE DIFFICULTY: Easy

TRAIL QUALITY: A simple dirt path, but quite muddy close to the falls

ROUND-TRIP DISTANCE: A little over 0.5 mile

ADMISSION: None, but donations to the Nature Conservancy are appreciated

TRIP REPORT & TIPS:

The waterfall at Falls Ridge Preserve is among the strangest I've ever seen. Visit the Nature Conservancy's website to learn more about this unique travertine falls.

From the parking area, follow the trail through a field, and after a little over 0.2 mile, turn right and follow up to the waterfall. There are two viewing areas here, and you'll note that the main flow of the waterfall is to the right, while the travertine buildup is most evident on the left.

Mill Creek Falls

LOCATION: Jefferson National Forest

ADDRESS/GPS FOR THE FALLS: Fenwick Mines Day-Use Area; 37° 33.984′ N, 80° 3.349′ W

DIRECTIONS: From New Castle, follow VA-615 for 5 miles to VA-611/Peaceful Valley Road. Turn left and follow for 0.2 mile, then turn right onto VA-685. Follow signs to Fenwick Mines Recreation Area.

WEBSITE: tinyurl.com/fenwickminesva

WATERWAY: Mill Creek

HEIGHT: About 12 feet **CREST:** Varies

NEAREST TOWN: New Castle

HIKE DIFFICULTY: Easy

TRAIL QUALITY: Fair

ROUND-TRIP DISTANCE: 1 mile

ADMISSION: None

TRIP REPORT & TIPS:

While probably not a destination waterfall, this little multiledge cascade is certainly worth a trip if you're nearby. The wheelchair-accessible path leads to an observation deck offering nice views of the falls, and a spur trail leads down to the stream where several nice vantage points await you.

From the parking area alongside the road, the crushed gravel trail is easy to follow, and at about 0.5 mile you'll reach the observation deck. The spur trail down to the creek is nearby and easy to find and follow. There are other trails in the park that are worthy of your time; the Wetlands Trail offers some nice scenes and would be a great spot for night photography.

Lace Falls

LOCATION: Natural Bridge State Park

ADDRESS/GPS FOR THE FALLS: 6477 South Lee Highway, Natural Bridge, VA 24578; 37° 38.074'N, 79° 33.279'W

DIRECTIONS: From I-81 South of Lexington, take exit 180 if northbound or 180A if southbound, and follow US-11 South for 3.2 miles to Natural Bridge. You can't miss the parking area and visitor center.

WEBSITE: tinyurl.com/naturalbridgeva

WATERWAY: Cedar Creek

HEIGHT: 35 feet **CREST:** Varies

NEAREST TOWN: Natural Bridge

HIKE DIFFICULTY: Easy

TRAIL QUALITY: A mix of pavement and crushed gravel

ROUND-TRIP DISTANCE: 2.2 miles

ADMISSION: $6 for ages 6–12; $8 for 13 and up

TRIP REPORT & TIPS:

While certainly not the highlight of your visit to Natural Bridge, Lace Falls is worth the additional walk. Natural Bridge is an amazing natural wonder, and I'm glad I finally had the opportunity to give it a look. Several exhibits along the way to Lace Falls are quite interesting, including the Monacan Village, a cave, and the Lost River. Lace Falls is nice and in a beautiful setting; bring your telephoto to this one, the observation area isn't very close to the falls.

Pay your fee at the visitor center, walk down the stairs, and exit the building. Follow the paved trail for 0.2 mile to the Natural Bridge. Continue for another 0.9 mile to the Lace Falls observation area to see the falls.

McGuirt Falls

LOCATION: Goshen Pass/Goshen Wildlife Management Area

ADDRESS/GPS FOR THE FALLS: VA-39/Maury River Road; 37° 55.617'N, 79° 27.417'W

DIRECTIONS: From Lexington, drive north and west on VA-39/Maury River Road for 13.7 miles to a small pulloff on the left. Don't block the gate; there are other areas to park if there is no room here.

WEBSITE: None

WATERWAY: Laurel Run

HEIGHT: A 25-foot run of cascades

CREST: Varies

NEAREST TOWN: Lexington

HIKE DIFFICULTY: Easy

TRAIL QUALITY: Forest road

ROUND-TRIP DISTANCE: 0.4 mile

ADMISSION: See page 11

TRIP REPORT & TIPS:

I dubbed this beautiful stair-step waterfall McGuirt Falls, since my good friend and fellow photographer Brent McGuirt introduced it to me. Brent was kind enough to take some time out of his busy schedule to share this and another waterfall with my buddy Kevin and me one fine spring day when we were in the area.

The hike to the falls is rated as easy, but the scramble down to the waterfall is a not-so-easy slip-and-slide through a rhododendron thicket. From the gate, simply follow the gravel road uphill for 0.2 mile, and then carefully scramble down to the stream and base of the falls.

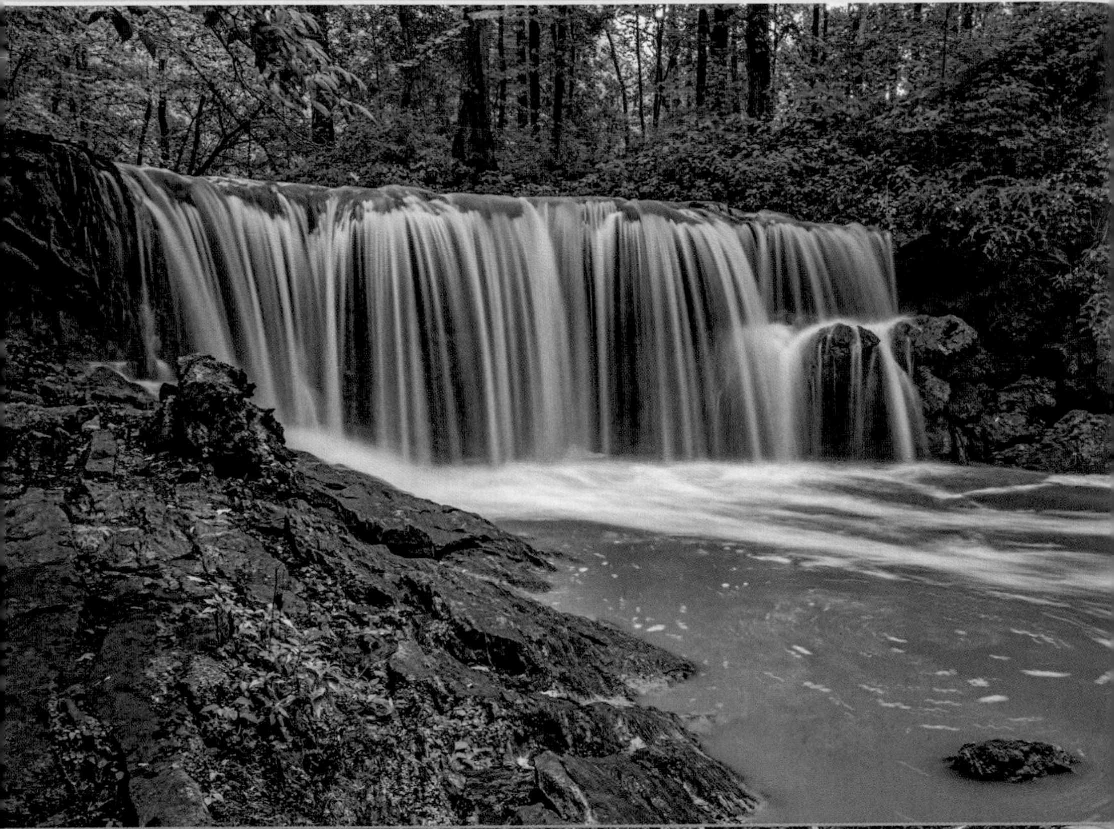

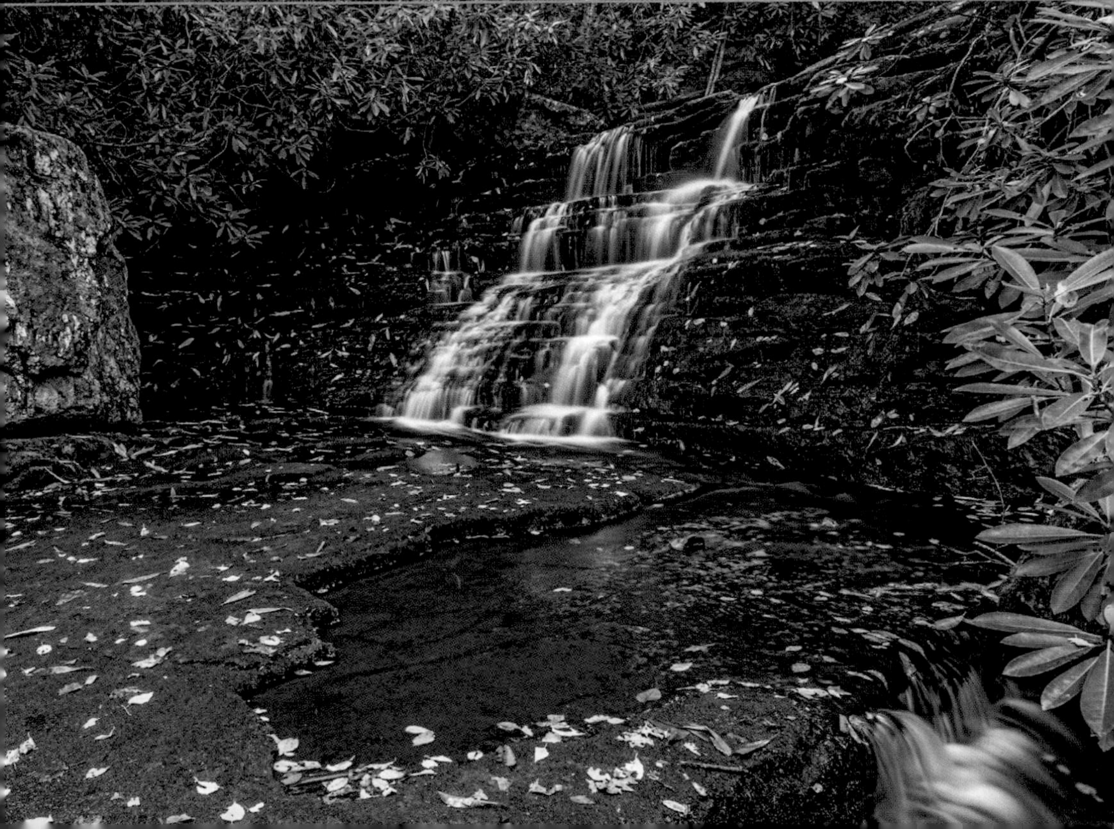

Folly Mills Falls

LOCATION: Cochran's Mill Road

ADDRESS/GPS FOR THE FALLS: SVA-871/ Cochran's Mill Road; 38° 5.865'N, 79° 5.985'W

DIRECTIONS: From I-64/I-81, take exit 217, then follow VA-654 (turn left if driving from Lexington, turn right if driving from Staunton), and follow for under 1 mile to US-11. Turn right onto US-11 and follow for 1.2 miles, then turn left onto VA-871/ Cochran's Mill Road and follow for 0.7 mile to a pullout on the left.

WEBSITE: None

WATERWAY: Folly Mills Creek

HEIGHT: 12 feet **CREST:** Varies

NEAREST TOWN: Mint Spring

HIKE DIFFICULTY: Easy

TRAIL QUALITY: Hard dirt-packed single-track

ROUND-TRIP DISTANCE: 0.2 mile

ADMISSION: None

TRIP REPORT & TIPS:

This little jewel is just minutes from I-64/I-81 near Staunton. It's such a neat waterfall, and the proximity to the interstate and the ease of access make this a great side trip if you're nearby. I visited a day after an inch of rain had fallen in the area, and the creek was moving fast.

From the roadside pullout, follow the well-worn path 0.1 mile to the waterfall. There is a short, steep incline about 20 yards into the hike, but some exposed tree roots will aid you in the climb. Near the falls there are a couple fallen trees on the path that you'll need to navigate under, over, or around, but doing so is not at all difficult.

Mill Creek Falls

LOCATION: Mill Creek Nature Park

ADDRESS/GPS FOR THE FALLS: 900 Northview Street, Narrows, VA 24124; 37° 18.135'N, 80° 47.702'W

DIRECTIONS: From US-460 in Narrows, cross the bridge over the New River into downtown Narrows, and follow MacArthur Lane for 0.2 mile. Turn left onto Main Street and follow for 0.4 mile, then turn right onto VA-652/Northview Street and follow for 1.2 miles to the park.

WEBSITE: tinyurl.com/millcreekparkva

WATERWAY: Mill Creek

HEIGHT: 15 feet **CREST:** Varies

NEAREST TOWN: Narrows

HIKE DIFFICULTY: Moderate

TRAIL QUALITY: Wide gravel road to start, then a rocky single-track with exposed roots

ROUND-TRIP DISTANCE: 2.4 miles

ADMISSION: None, but donations appreciated

TRIP REPORT & TIPS:

Mill Creek is a wonderful mountain stream full of great little cascades and waterfalls.

From the gate just beyond the trail kiosk, follow the Butternut Trail gradually uphill to a historic dam where the trail then becomes single-track. At a little over 0.4 mile from the gate, the Butternut Trail veers off to the left, and you'll pick up the Waterfall Trail to the right. At around the 1-mile mark, you'll reach Mercy Run, crossing it and then bearing right, downhill. At the 1.1-mile mark, you'll reach a spur trail that leads you steeply down to the waterfall.

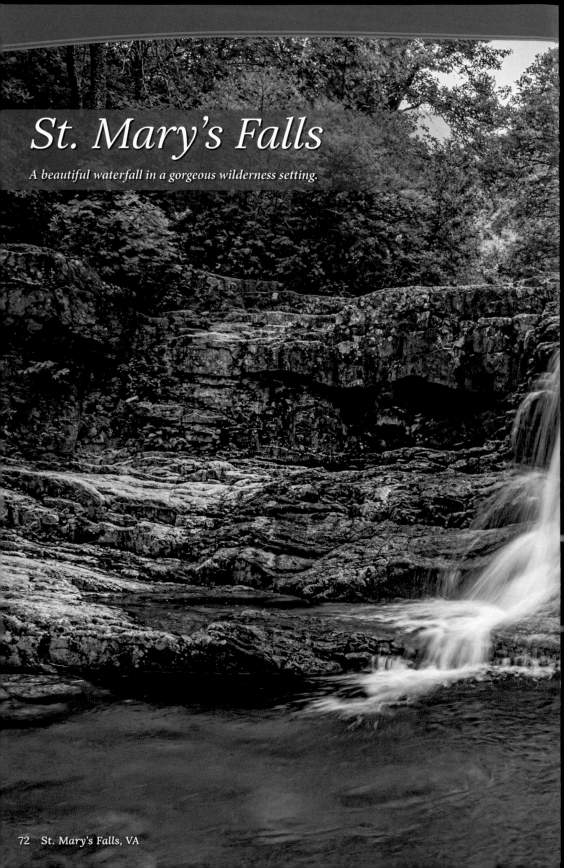

St. Mary's Falls

A beautiful waterfall in a gorgeous wilderness setting.

St. Mary's River

St. Mary's Falls

Part of the Saint Mary's Wilderness, you'll access Saint Mary's Falls by travelling along an old railroad grade that once served manganese mines.

LOCATION: George Washington National Forest

ADDRESS/GPS FOR THE FALLS: St. Mary's Road; 37° 55.771' N, 79° 6.42' W

DIRECTIONS: Leave the Blue Ridge Parkway at Tye River Gap (mile 27.2), and follow VA-56 West for 4.3 miles. Turn right onto VA-608 and follow for 2.1 miles, then turn right to stay on VA-608 and follow for 0.3 mile. Turn right onto St. Mary's Road, and follow for 1.3 miles to the parking area.

WEBSITE: None

WATERWAY: Saint Mary's River

HEIGHT: 15 feet **CREST:** Varies

NEAREST TOWN: Vesuvius

HIKE DIFFICULTY: Moderate, due to stream crossings

TRAIL QUALITY: A mixed bag with sections of hard dirt, areas of exposed roots, rock fields, and then you have the river crossings

ROUND-TRIP DISTANCE: 4.6 miles

ADMISSION: None

TRIP REPORT & TIPS:

This very popular Virginia hike and waterfall has been on my radar for years, and I finally made the trek with my friend Kevin on a pleasant summer day. The area had received around an inch of rain a couple days prior, and we had hoped the water level would be good, but it was a bit lower than I would prefer. However, it was hard to complain when surrounded by such gorgeous scenery with a beautiful waterfall in front of us.

Saint Mary's Falls is located in the Saint Mary's Wilderness area of George Washington National Forest. At just under 10,000 acres, Saint Mary's is the largest designated wilderness area in Virginia. The wilderness designation means just that; you'll be in the wilderness, with no trail signage or trail blazes. Don't let that scare you off, though. The hike is easy, with very little elevation gain. The only reason I gave the hike a moderate difficulty rating is because of the stream crossings. At low water level, they aren't difficult at all and weren't hard to locate. However, I'd proceed with extreme caution during high and swift water conditions; those stream crossings will be very tricky and a few of them hard to locate. With no blazes, you might think the trail would be hard to follow, but with its popularity, it's more like a hiker's superhighway—very easy to follow. There are a few spur trails leading to fishing holes and/or camping spots, so if you do get out of sorts, just remember to always follow the river. At no point should you follow any trails leading far away from the stream.

From the trail kiosk, follow the St. Mary's Trail upriver, and at the 1-mile mark, you'll reach a trail junction. Take the right fork to the river, make your first stream crossing, and rejoin the trail. At 1.2 miles, you'll reach another trail junction; stay straight and continue paralleling the river. You'll reach the next stream crossing at around the 1.3-mile mark and the final stream crossing at about the 2-mile mark. You should now be on the right side of the stream (looking upriver), and in another 0.2 mile you'll arrive at a ledge overlooking the falls.

Crabtree Falls

Crabtree Falls is one of the tallest sets of waterfalls east of the Mississippi River.

Middle Crabtree Falls

Crabtree Falls

Once at the top of the Upper Falls, you'll be rewarded with an amazing view of the Tye River Gorge.

LOCATION: George Washington National Forest

ADDRESS/GPS FOR THE FALLS: VA-56/Crabtree Falls Highway; 37° 51.006′ N, 79° 4.661′ W

DIRECTIONS: Exit the Blue Ridge Parkway at Tye River Gap, between miles 27-28, then turn left onto VA-56 East/Crabtree Falls Highway. Follow for almost 7 miles, and turn right into the parking area.

WEBSITE: tinyurl.com/crabtreefallsva

WATERWAY: Crabtree Creek

HEIGHT: Between all three drops, over 1,000 feet **CREST:** Varies

NEAREST TOWN: Montbellow

HIKE DIFFICULTY: Easy to moderate

TRAIL QUALITY: A nice paved walkway to the lower falls, with stairs, railings, wooden walkways, and a rocky, rooted dirt path beyond

ROUND-TRIP DISTANCE: 3.2 miles to the base of the Upper Falls and back, or 3.4 miles to the top of the Upper Falls and back

ADMISSION: $3 per vehicle

TRIP REPORT & TIPS:

Crabtree Falls is often advertised as "the tallest waterfall in Virginia", but as I hadn't visited it, I didn't know what to expect. I'd classify Crabtree Falls as a series of individual, significant waterfalls or drops. The hike begins at the parking lot. Follow the level, paved pathway for 0.2 mile to the viewing platform of what I'll call the Lower Falls. The platform allows for several nice compositions of the Lower Falls, with faint glimpses of another significant drop upstream. The trail breaks away from the drop above the Lower Falls, so it appeared to be more of slide than a true cascade of falling water. From the Lower Falls viewing platform, continue your hike upstream, passing a very nice stream scene. The hike begins to enter into the moderate category here, and at 0.4 mile you'll reach a staircase that leads to a nice view of what I've called the Middle Falls. I took the time to make some images here, but I found that I liked the images of this drop from a vantage point at about the 1-mile mark. The trail leads you away from the creek at times, but you won't be out of earshot of Crabtree Creek, especially during periods of high water. The trail was a bit muddy due to the recent rainfall, but it wasn't too difficult to navigate, due to steps along the steepest sections. From here, continue along the trail for another 0.6 mile to the base of the Upper Falls. At 1.6 miles, you'll reach the base of the Upper Falls at a large boulder on the creek side of the trail. Note: There is a sign at the beginning of the hike stating that 30 people have died due to falling after wandering off the trail. Please stay on the trail, or you'll be a statistic.

Upper Crabtree Falls

Apple Orchard Falls

This is one of Virginia's tallest and more spectacular waterfalls.

Apple Orchard Falls

Apple Orchard Mountain was named for the nature of the northern red oak forests dominating the mountain. The weather is so harsh on the upper elevations that the trees have a stunted appearance, like they have been pruned, resembling an orchard.

LOCATION: Apple Orchard Falls Trail

ADDRESS/GPS FOR THE FALLS: Blue Ridge Parkway–Sunset Field Overlook; 37° 30.998′ N, 79°31′56.99″ W

DIRECTIONS: Find the Sunset Field Overlook Parking Area on the west side of the parkway at mile 78.4.

WEBSITE: tinyurl.com/appleorchardva

WATERWAY: Tributary of North Creek

HEIGHT: 85 feet   **CREST:** Varies

NEAREST TOWN: Arcadia

HIKE DIFFICULTY: Moderate to strenuous

TRAIL QUALITY: Rocky, with a few stream crossings and a bunch of steps on the final descent to the falls

ROUND-TRIP DISTANCE: 2.8 miles

ADMISSION: None

TRIP REPORT & TIPS:

My friend Kevin and I visited Apple Orchard Falls on a rainy early-spring day. We started our hike from the Sunset Field overlook on the parkway, and it was a steady downhill hike most of the way, which of course means a steady uphill return hike with an elevation gain of over 1,000 feet. There's a nice little bonus falls that you'll see after crossing a footbridge at just over the 1-mile mark. From there, the trail leads you away from the stream, and in a short distance it curves back toward the creek. The trail then goes sharply down the mountain, with over 100 steps assisting you in the descent; be careful if the steps are wet, they were quite slick on our visit. At the bottom of the steps, you'll reach an elaborate boardwalk system leading you a short distance to the base of the falls.

From the trailhead, begin your descent on the Apple Orchard Falls Trail. At 0.3 mile you'll reach a trail junction; stay straight and continue on the Apple Orchard Falls Trail. At 0.7 mile you'll reach another trail intersection; follow the signs to stay on the Apple Orchard Falls Trail. At 1.1 miles, cross the footbridge and look upstream for the little bonus waterfall. Continue on the trail as it leads away from the creek and then curves back to the steps and the steep descent to the base of the falls at 1.4 miles.

If you want to eliminate a lot of the elevation gain, you can access a lower trailhead off of Forest Road 812 and Forest Road 3034. From Sunset Field Overlook, follow Forest Road 812 for 2.8 miles, then turn left onto Forest Road 3034 and follow for 2.1 miles to the end of the road; the trailhead is to the left of the kiosk, and it is a 0.75-mile hike with an elevation gain of around 650 feet to Apple Orchard Falls. You can also access this from I-81 by taking the Arcadia exit (exit 168). Follow VA-614 for 2.9 miles through Arcadia to Forest Road 59 and turn left. Go 3 miles, just past North Creek Campground, and turn left onto Forest Road 768. Next, turn right on Forest Road 812 and go about 3.4 miles to Forest Road 3034. Turn right and park at the end of the road.

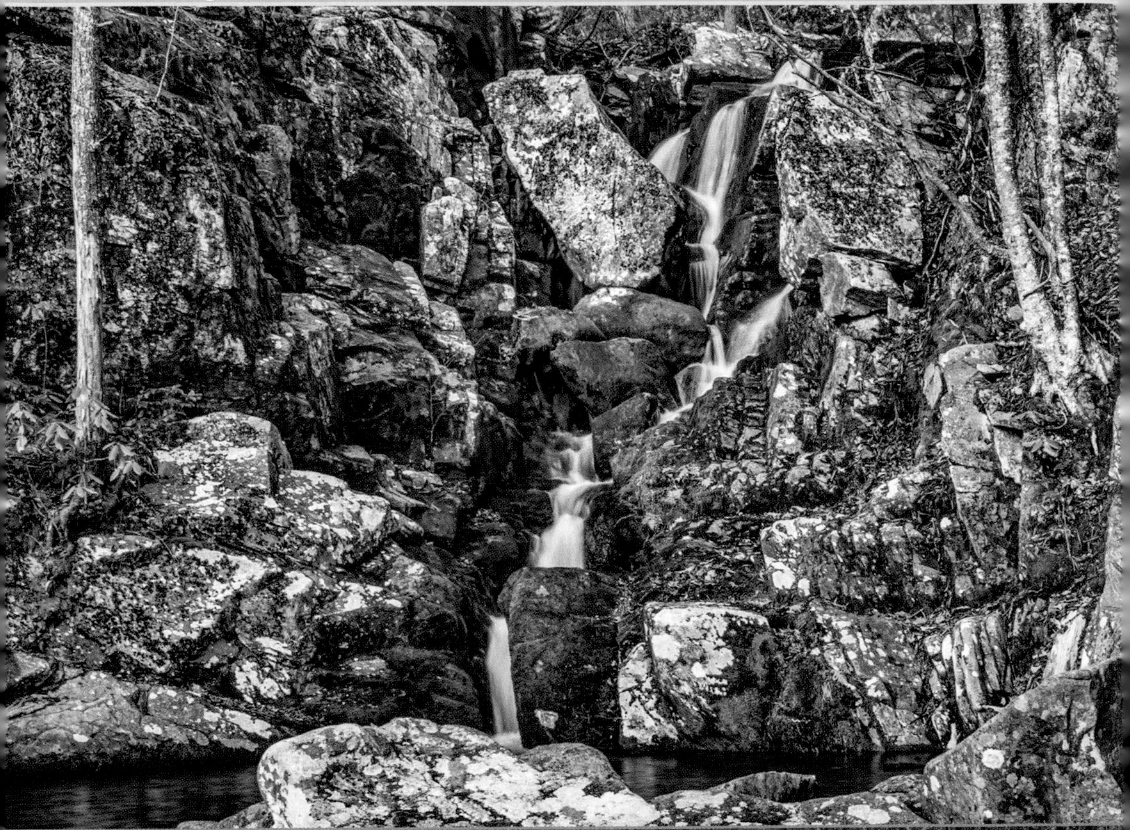

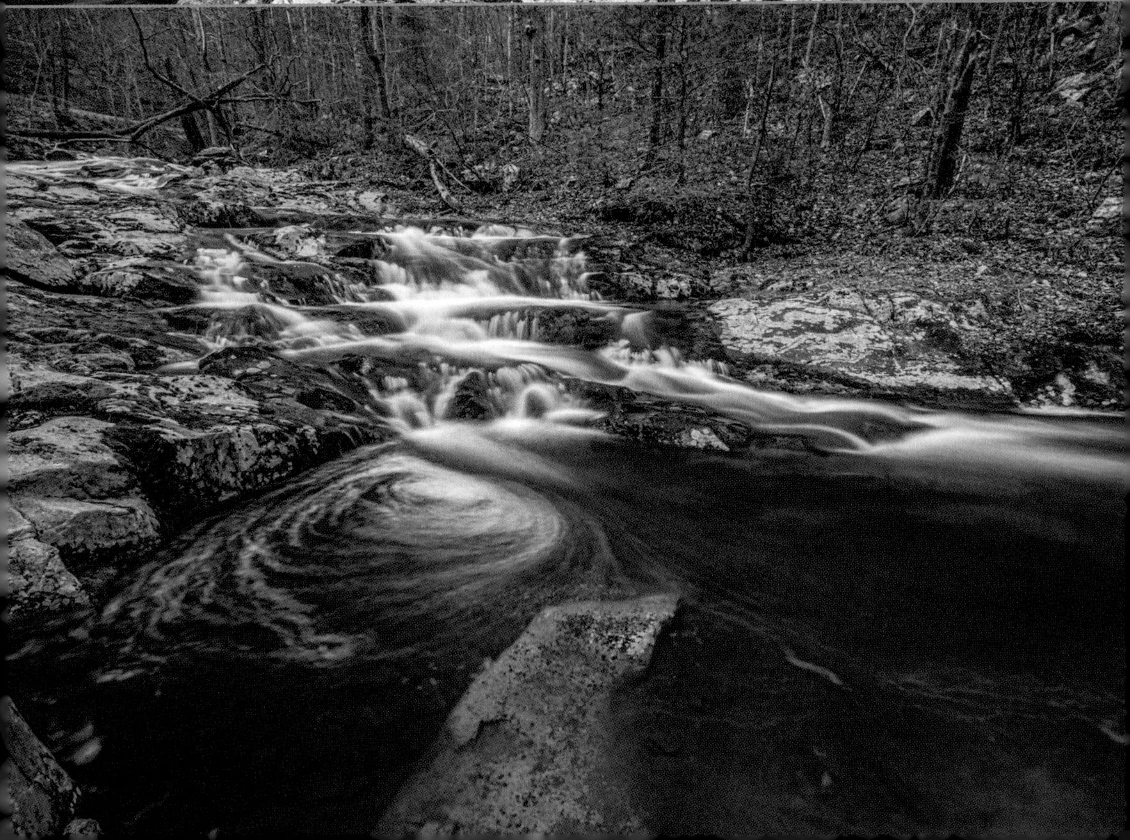

White Rock Falls

LOCATION: White Rock Falls Trail

ADDRESS/GPS FOR THE FALLS: The Slacks Overlook Parking Area; Blue Ridge Parkway Mile 19.9; 37° 54.15'N, 79° 3.281'W

DIRECTIONS: The Slacks Overlook Parking Area is on the west side of the parkway. From the parking area, walk across the parkway and turn left, heading north along the roadside. You'll find the trailhead about 0.1 mile from the parking area.

WEBSITE: None

WATERWAY: White Rock Creek

HEIGHT: 25 feet **CREST:** Varies

NEAREST TOWN: Montebello

HIKE DIFFICULTY: Moderate

TRAIL QUALITY: Good, easy to follow, with footbridges and crude steps; some rocky terrain

ROUND-TRIP DISTANCE: 1.2 miles

ADMISSION: None

TRIP REPORT & TIPS:

This was an enjoyable hike on an easy-to-follow trail. At about 0.4 mile from the trailhead, you'll reach a section of rock outcrops with beautiful views. From the outcrop, there is a shortcut down to the waterfall spur trail, but it requires a steep scramble between two large boulders. We opted to follow the trail, which in about 0.1 mile or so takes a sharp left and descends to the base of the outcrops. The main trail switches back to the right, while the spur trail to White Rock Falls stays straight along the base of the outcrop. Follow the spur trail a short distance down to the falls. On the return, Kevin and I decided to take the shortcut by climbing up through the two boulders; it's easy to see the route through the boulders and not that difficult of a climb.

Box Spring Falls

LOCATION: Irish Creek Road

ADDRESS/GPS FOR THE FALLS: VA-603/Irish Creek Road; 37° 49.766'N, 79° 12.467'W

DIRECTIONS: At mile 27.2 on the Blue Ridge Parkway, southbound travelers should turn left (northbound travelers turn right) onto VA-813/Whetstone Ridge Road and follow it for a few hundred feet. Then turn right onto VA-603/Irish Creek Road and follow it for 5.2 miles.

WEBSITE: None

WATERWAY: Irish Creek

HEIGHT: 15- to 20-foot cascading run

CREST: Varies

NEAREST TOWN: Montebello

HIKE DIFFICULTY: Roadside view or scramble

TRAIL QUALITY: Poor, due to trash on the short scramble down to the creek

ROUND-TRIP DISTANCE: 100 feet, if doing the scramble

ADMISSION: None

TRIP REPORT & TIPS:

This is another waterfall that my good friend Brent led my buddy Kevin and me to on one early-spring afternoon. It's quite pretty, but unfortunately there is a bit of trash along the bank, including a few box springs. I should note that while there weren't any "No Trespassing" signs above the falls, there were some about 50 yards down the road, so if you do see posted signs during your visit, shoot your photos from the road.

Wigwam Falls

LOCATION: Blue Ridge Parkway

ADDRESS/GPS FOR THE FALLS: Yankee Horse Ridge Parking Area, mile 34.4; 37° 48.514′ N, 79° 10.734′ W

DIRECTIONS: The Yankee Horse Ridge Parking Area is at mile 34.4 on the east side of the Parkway.

WEBSITE: None

WATERWAY: A branch of Wigwam Creek

HEIGHT: A sliding cascade of about 25 feet

CREST: Varies

NEAREST TOWN: Montebello

HIKE DIFFICULTY: Easy

TRAIL QUALITY: Good, hard-packed surface with some exposed roots

ROUND-TRIP DISTANCE: About 0.1 mile

ADMISSION: None

TRIP REPORT & TIPS:

The hike up to Wigwam Falls is a nice way to stretch your legs on a very short walk up to the falls and catch a glimpse of history in the process. From the Yankee Horse Ridge Parking Area, named after a Civil War era Union soldier's horse falling near here and having to be put down, climb a few steps up to the trail. The trail is actually a short section of reconstructed narrow-gauge railroad track of the old Irish Creek Railway. There is also a bit of history on the logging efforts of that era. Continue along the track, and look for a trail to the left that leads up to the falls. Wigwam Falls is in a beautiful setting, surrounded by boulders and ferns, and the water slides down a ledge laden with moss.

Panther Creek Falls

LOCATION: George Washington National Forest

ADDRESS/GPS FOR THE FALLS: Panther Falls Road; 37° 43.134′ N, 79° 17.403′ W

DIRECTIONS: From mile 45.6 on the Blue Ridge Parkway, follow US-60 east for 0.1 mile, and turn right onto Forest Road 315/Panther Falls Road. Follow this gravel road for 3.1 miles to a small parking area on the left.

WEBSITE: None

WATERWAY: Pedlar River

HEIGHT: 15 feet **CREST:** Varies

NEAREST TOWN: Buena Vista

HIKE DIFFICULTY: Easy, with a slippery scramble down to the stream

TRAIL QUALITY: Good, with a few muddy/boggy sections

ROUND-TRIP DISTANCE: 0.35 mile

ADMISSION: None

TRIP REPORT & TIPS:

Although Kevin and I visited this waterfall under a cloudless sky, the late-afternoon sun was already off of the stream. With the sun dipping below the mountains, it highlighted the forest on the opposite side of the Pedlar River and created a nice colorful reflection in the water. With such a large pool area below the falls, it's easy to see why this is a popular swimming spot in the summer months.

From the parking area, descend from the road to the river, then bear right and follow the somewhat soggy path to the top of the falls. Several well-worn paths lead you to various vantage points to photograph the falls.

Upper Statons Creek Falls

LOCATION: George Washington National Forest

ADDRESS/GPS FOR THE FALLS: Fiddlers Green Way; 37° 46.099' N, 79° 14.183' W

DIRECTIONS: At mile 45.6 on the Blue Ridge Parkway, follow US-60 east for 3.3 miles, then turn left on VA-605/Pedlar River Road. Follow for 2.1 miles, and at the fork, bear right onto VA-633/Fiddlers Green Way. Follow the gravel road for a little over 1 mile to the obvious pullout on the right. The upper section of the falls is just across the road.

WEBSITE: None

WATERWAY: Statons Creek

HEIGHT: A double drop of 15 to 20 feet

CREST: Varies

NEAREST TOWN: Buena Vista

HIKE DIFFICULTY: Roadside

TRAIL QUALITY: Roadside, or a short scramble to the base

ROUND-TRIP DISTANCE: Roadside

ADMISSION: None

TRIP REPORT & TIPS:

I first saw Upper and Lower Statons Creek Falls several years ago during a trip my wife and I took to visit good friends in nearby Lexington. My friend Brent and I were driving back from a sunrise hike on the Appalachian Trail when he decided to make the short side trip here. We found it with little water flow that morning, so I opted not to take the any photographs. A few years later, my buddy Kevin and I caught Statons Creek with much better water flow. Roadside shots are doable here, but I scrambled the short distance down to the pool area below the falls.

Lower Statons Creek Falls

LOCATION: George Washington National Forest

ADDRESS/GPS FOR THE FALLS: Fiddlers Green Way; 37° 46.104' N, 79° 14.201' W

DIRECTIONS: At mile 45.6 on the Blue Ridge Parkway, follow US-60 east for 3.3 miles, then turn left on VA-605/Pedlar River Road. Follow for 2.1 miles, and at the fork, bear right onto VA-633/Fiddlers Green Way. Follow the gravel road for a little over 1 mile to the obvious pullout on the right. From the Upper Falls, very carefully work your way downstream on a worn and easy-to-follow path.

WEBSITE: None

WATERWAY: Statons Creek

HEIGHT: About 100 feet over a few separate drops

CREST: Varies

NEAREST TOWN: Buena Vista

HIKE DIFFICULTY: Strenuous

TRAIL QUALITY: None; bushwhacking a path down a steep, slippery hillside

ROUND-TRIP DISTANCE: 200 feet

ADMISSION: None

TRIP REPORT & TIPS:

While the path down to the base is easy to follow, it is deceptively slick, due to vegetation obscuring the wet rock ledge you're descending. Make this trek with extreme care, as there have been a few deaths here due to falls. There are a couple vantage points about midway down that offer closer views of the top section of the upper falls, but I liked working in the entire drop from just beyond the pool area.

Fallingwater Cascades

LOCATION: Blue Ridge Parkway

ADDRESS/GPS FOR THE FALLS: Mile 83.1 on the Blue Ridge Parkway; 37° 28.599′ N, 79° 34.887′ W

DIRECTIONS: The parking area for Fallingwater Cascades is on the west side of the parkway at mile 83.1, north of Peaks of Otter Lodge.

WEBSITE: tinyurl.com/fallingwaterva

WATERWAY: Fallingwater Creek

HEIGHT: 100 feet, over two sliding drops

CREST: Varies

NEAREST TOWN: Buchanan

HIKE DIFFICULTY: Moderate

TRAIL QUALITY: Rocky, with some exposed roots, but easy to follow

ROUND-TRIP DISTANCE: 1 mile

ADMISSION: None

TRIP REPORT & TIPS:

I've yet to catch this stream with heavy water flow, but on my most recent visit, at least there was a decent amount. The hike down to the two main slide sections is pleasant, with nice views of Flat Top and Sharp Top Mountains. At around 0.3 mile, you'll cross a footbridge over Fallingwater Creek and continue your descent to the two main drops. At around 0.4 mile, there is a spur path that leads you to the base of the first big drop, which is the image I've featured for this listing. Back on the main trail, continue your descent another 0.1 mile to the base of the final drop. On my last visit, a large tree had fallen on the stream, marring the view a bit. The trail continues on as a loop, but I've always re-traced my steps back to the parking area.

Bent Mountain Falls

LOCATION: Bottom Creek Gorge Preserve

ADDRESS/GPS FOR THE FALLS: Bottom Creek Gorge Preserve; 37° 7.067′ N, 80° 10.983′ W

DIRECTIONS: At mile 135.9, exit the Blue Ridge Parkway and follow for 0.3 mile, then turn left onto US-221 South and follow for 0.6 mile. Then turn right onto VA-644/County Line Road. At 1.1 miles, the road forks. Bear to the right on VA-669/ Patterson Drive. After 0.8 mile, continue straight on Route 669. (Don't turn right on Bottom Creek Road/Route 607.) After 1.5 miles, you'll come to a "Y" intersection. Bear slightly right, staying on Route 669. Soon you"ll be driving alongside Bottom Creek. After 1.3 miles, cross a small bridge. Look for the Preserve sign on the left. Turn left at the sign, taking the gravel driveway to the gate.

WEBSITE: tinyurl.com/bottomcreekva

WATERWAY: Camp Creek

HEIGHT: 200-plus feet **CREST:** Varies

NEAREST TOWN: Bent Mountain

HIKE DIFFICULTY: Easy, but a few steep ascents

TRAIL QUALITY: Easy to follow, with some rocks/ roots along the way

ROUND-TRIP DISTANCE: 3.2 miles

ADMISSION: None

TRIP REPORT & TIPS:

While certainly 200 feet tall, Bent Mountain Falls is only visible from across the gorge. From the parking area, go through the gate and follow for 0.46 mile to the trail kiosk. The red-blazed Johnston Trail offers the most direct access and is easy to follow, well marked, and scenic. The last 0.3 mile is a mild descent to the viewing area.

Overall Run Falls

A waterfall with a view!

Overall Run Falls

Overall Run Falls is the tallest waterfall in the park, but it is on a small stream and is one of the first to dry up; be sure to visit in the spring or after a heavy rain.

LOCATION: North District, Shenandoah National Park

ADDRESS/GPS FOR THE FALLS: Skyline Drive; 38° 46.954′ N, 78° 17.668′ W

DIRECTIONS: The parking area is on Skyline Drive, just south of the Hogback Overlook, at mile marker 21.1.

WEBSITE: tinyurl.com/overallsnp

WATERWAY: Overall Run

HEIGHT: 93 feet **CREST:** Varies

NEAREST TOWN: Front Royal

HIKE DIFFICULTY: Moderate, with a climb of over 1,800 feet on the way back to the parking area

TRAIL QUALITY: A wide, easy-to-follow dirt path

ROUND-TRIP DISTANCE: 5.7 miles

ADMISSION: For information on admission fees, please visit tinyurl.com/snpfees

TRIP REPORT & TIPS:

It's not often that I come away from a waterfall with low water flow feeling a sense of a successful shoot. I had hoped to visit Overall Run Falls during the spring, so that I would see the falls in all of its glory, but I didn't make it there until early summer. The amazing and expansive views from the rocky overlooks were spectacular and more than made up for the lackluster flow on Overall Run. My friend Kevin was with me again, and in addition to the gorgeous views from the overlooks, we were treated to a quick glimpse of a beautiful black bear just off the trail, about halfway through our return hike. There is a smaller waterfall (compared to the big falls) about 0.2 mile before reaching the overlook. I've seen it called Twin Falls, and at 25 feet or so, it looks like it would be a great waterfall to photograph with decent water flow.

From the lower end of the parking area, locate the trailhead for the Appalachian Trail, and follow for 0.4 mile. At the intersection with the Tuscarora-Overall Run Trail, turn right onto the Tuscarora-Overall Run Trail, and follow for about 2.4 miles down to the falls. There is a rather steep descent near the overlook, but for the most part, the downhill portion is gradual. There is an alternate route from the Matthews Arm Campground that shortens the distance a bit, and I have read that noncampers can park at the amphitheater parking lot and follow the Traces Trail to the Tuscarora Trail. However, on our visit, the campground was closed for some reason, so we were unable to try the Traces Trail route.

Note: If you enter the park via the North Entrance, the first waterfall on Skyline Drive is actually Lands Run Falls, pictured and described on page 108. Due to this book's format, the more-popular Overall Run Falls, and others, are listed first.

The Falls of Whiteoak Canyon

One of Shenandoah National Park's most popular destinations.

Whiteoak Falls #2

The Falls of Whiteoak Canyon

A challenging, yet rewarding hike awaits you in Whiteoak Canyon.

LOCATION: Central District, Shenandoah National Park

ADDRESS/GPS FOR THE FALLS: Skyline Drive; Upper Falls: 38° 33.8′ N, 78° 21.8′ W; directions to the other falls follows

DIRECTIONS: The parking area is on the east side of Skyline Drive at mile 42.6.

WEBSITE: tinyurl.com/whiteoakva

WATERWAY: Whiteoak Run

HEIGHT: Upper Falls: 86 feet **CREST:** Varies

NEAREST TOWN: Elkton

HIKE DIFFICULTY: Strenuous, especially near the end, due to steep and rocky descents

TRAIL QUALITY: The upper portion of the trail is gravel, but then it becomes quite rocky; it is very slick during wet weather

ROUND-TRIP DISTANCE: 7.5 miles

ADMISSION: For information on admission fees, please visit tinyurl.com/snpfees

TRIP REPORT & TIPS:

I love multiwaterfall hikes, and my friend Kevin and I were excited to see all the waterfalls in Whiteoak Canyon. We couldn't have timed our visit any better. We were there in early spring during a very rainy period, and in fact, it rained on us for most of the hike.

The online sources I consulted listed six waterfalls in Whiteoak Canyon, but we saw several more, as well as some beautiful stream scenes with small cascades. In this book, I'm also featuring six waterfalls, but a couple of them aren't the ones I saw during my research. The waterfalls I've listed are ones I could safely access with the high water flow and very slick conditions. If you're there during normal water flow and the access is safe, you should definitely explore all the user-created paths to each of the waterfalls you'll see or hear along the hike—I know I'll be back again to see them all!

I'll go ahead and be honest with you here: I'm not a huge fan of strenuous and steep uphill hikes, and neither is my friend Kevin. We began our hike at the trailhead, which is located at the north end of the parking area. But to avoid the return hike uphill, and to maximize our time in the park, we set up a shuttle. We left Kevin's vehicle at the lower parking area and drove my vehicle back up to the trailhead on Skyline Drive.

The trail begins innocently enough and is a pleasant stroll through a beautiful forest. After about 2 miles into the hike, you'll reach the Upper Falls, with a dramatic view from a rocky outcropping. I carefully made my way along the extremely slick and uneven surface to try to capture as much of the waterfall as I could. It was surrounded by a light fog that made for a nice moody image. From here to the lower falls, you'll be going downhill—a lot!

Whiteoak Falls #3

Whiteoak Falls #4

Whiteoak Falls #5

Whiteoak Falls #6

TRIP REPORT (CONTINUED): It was at this point that Kevin and I remarked that we were glad we didn't have to hike back up, a remark we repeated quite often.

From the Upper Falls, follow the trail for about 0.3 mile to the second waterfall, where a user-created path leads you down to this 60-foot beauty. Back up on the trail, follow for less than 0.1 mile to another user-created path down to the third waterfall I've featured. This one is a neat 15-footer that seemed to appear out of nowhere from the deep green forest.

The fourth waterfall I photographed was again found after hiking less than 0.1 mile. After wading a short section of the stream and crawling over a large fallen tree, I really enjoyed shooting this little one. It had great characteristics, and I loved how the water cascaded through the frame. Back on the trail and a short distance from the fourth waterfall, you'll reach a viewing point for the fifth waterfall I photographed. We moved along down the steep trail to a better vantage point to photograph this waterfall, and in the featured photo, I included a little portion of a side stream crashing into Whiteoak Run.

From this point, we made our way along the trail, twisting and turning steeply down the canyon about 0.4 mile to Lower Whiteoak Falls. This 60-footer was my favorite of the six I photographed, and I spent a lot of time here, working on every conceivable angle. If you're doing the round-trip hike, here's where you turn back around and make your way back up to the trailhead on Skyline Drive. But if you're doing the shuttle, continue hiking along Whiteoak Run for a little over 1 mile to the lower parking area.

If you wish to set up a shuttle, or hike uphill first, the lower parking area is on Chad Berry Lane in Syria, VA. From the Thornton Gap Entrance Station on Skyline Drive, follow VA-211 East for almost 8 miles to Sperryville, then turn right onto VA-522 South for 0.8 mile. Turn right on VA-231, and follow for 10.2 miles to Etlan. Turn right on VA-643, and follow for 4.5 miles, then turn right onto VA-600 and follow for 3.5 miles to the parking area.

Dark Hollow Falls

A Shenandoah National Park must-see waterfall!

Dark Hollow Falls

Arrive here early to beat the crowds.

LOCATION: Central District, Shenandoah National Park

ADDRESS/GPS FOR THE FALLS: Skyline Drive; 38° 31.15′ N, 78° 25.405′ W

DIRECTIONS: The parking area is on the east side of Skyline Drive at mile 50.7.

WEBSITE: tinyurl.com/darkhollowsnp

WATERWAY: Hogcamp Branch

HEIGHT: A cascading series of falls totaling about 50 feet **CREST:** Varies

NEAREST TOWN: Elkton

HIKE DIFFICULTY: Moderate, due to steep descent/ascent

TRAIL QUALITY: Easy to follow gravel and dirt path

ROUND-TRIP DISTANCE: 1.5 miles

ADMISSION: For information on admission fees, please visit tinyurl.com/snpfees

TRIP REPORT & TIPS:

Kevin and I caught Dark Hollow Falls at the perfect time. Great water flow, a light rain, fog, and the new greens of spring made for an enchanting scene. This waterfall is very popular, due to its proximity to Big Meadows and its relatively short hiking distance, so we arrived early in the morning in hopes of missing most of the crowd. There were still about a dozen or so vehicles at the parking area when we got there, and there were people arriving and departing the entire time we were there. We drove by the parking area later that day, and then during an early summer trip, and saw that it was overflowing with vehicles, so again, it's best to get there as early as possible. You can combine this hike with the Rose River Falls (page 110) hike, and we met a few folks who were doing just that. Kevin and I opted not to do the circuit, but if you do, pick up a park map. Shenandoah National Park utilizes concrete trail-marker posts with directional information at trailheads and trail intersections, so the circuit hike is marked and easy to follow.

From the trailhead at the north end of the parking area, descend and you'll cross Hogcamp Branch and will follow along the creek for most of the hike. Even with all the rain the area received prior to and during our visit, Kevin and I wondered if the hike was going to be worthwhile, since at the beginning of the hike, Hogcamp Branch was basically just a trickle. But it picks up plenty of water along the way, and at around the 0.5-mile mark of the hike, you'll start to see some small waterfalls and stream scenes that are worthy of shooting. At the 0.6-mile mark, you'll reach the top of the falls, and the trail veers away from the stream for a short distance, before winding its way back steeply toward the stream and depositing you at the base of the falls at a little over the 0.7-mile mark. Be sure to go downstream just a bit, where you'll see a beautiful 8-foot cascade that will make a great foreground feature, with Dark Hollow Falls upstream. You won't be able to get the entire run into the frame, but it does make for a fantastic image. If you're not doing the Rose River circuit, retrace your steps back up to the parking area on Skyline Drive.

Cedar Run #1

Cedar Run #2

Waterfalls on Cedar Run

LOCATION: Central District, Shenandoah National Park

ADDRESS/GPS FOR THE FALLS: Skyline Drive; 38° 32.552′ N, 78° 22.073′ W

DIRECTIONS: The parking area is found at mile 45.6 on the east side of Skyline Drive.

WEBSITE: None

WATERWAY: Cedar Run

HEIGHT: The Cedar Run Slide is a 60-foot slide, while the second waterfall featured is a 25-footer that falls through a narrow slot **CREST:** Varies

NEAREST TOWN: Elkton

HIKE DIFFICULTY: Strenuous, with an elevation gain of around 1,800 feet

TRAIL QUALITY: Quite rocky most of the route

ROUND-TRIP DISTANCE: 4.5 miles

ADMISSION: For information on admission fees, please visit tinyurl.com/snpfees

TRIP REPORT & TIPS:

If the water levels are good, you can spend a lot of time on Cedar Run, which is home to four significant waterfalls and several beautiful small cascades. Kevin and I set up another shuttle and hiked the brutal Cedar Run Trail downhill from the parking area on Skyline Drive. As opposed to our Whiteoak Canyon hike several weeks prior, we visited Cedar Run when water levels were low.

The trailhead is located at the parking area. From the trailhead, follow the trail downhill, and at around the 1.3-mile mark, you'll cross Cedar Run at a small waterfall with a nice pool area. You'll arrive at the Cedar Run Slide at the 1.5-mile mark, and be prepared to share the slide with other folks if you're there in the warmer months. Waterfall #2 is 0.2 mile from the slide, and you'll need to scramble down from the trail to get a good shot. There are a couple more significant waterfalls farther on downstream; the third waterfall is at the 1.9-mile mark and the fourth is at the 2.2-mile mark. They require some serious scrambling, and with the low water flow it just wasn't worth the effort. If you're not doing a shuttle, retrace your steps back up the trail to the parking area. If you're doing a shuttle, continue 0.2 mile and you'll cross Cedar Run at another small waterfall. Then follow the trail for 0.7 mile to the Lower Whiteoak Parking Area.

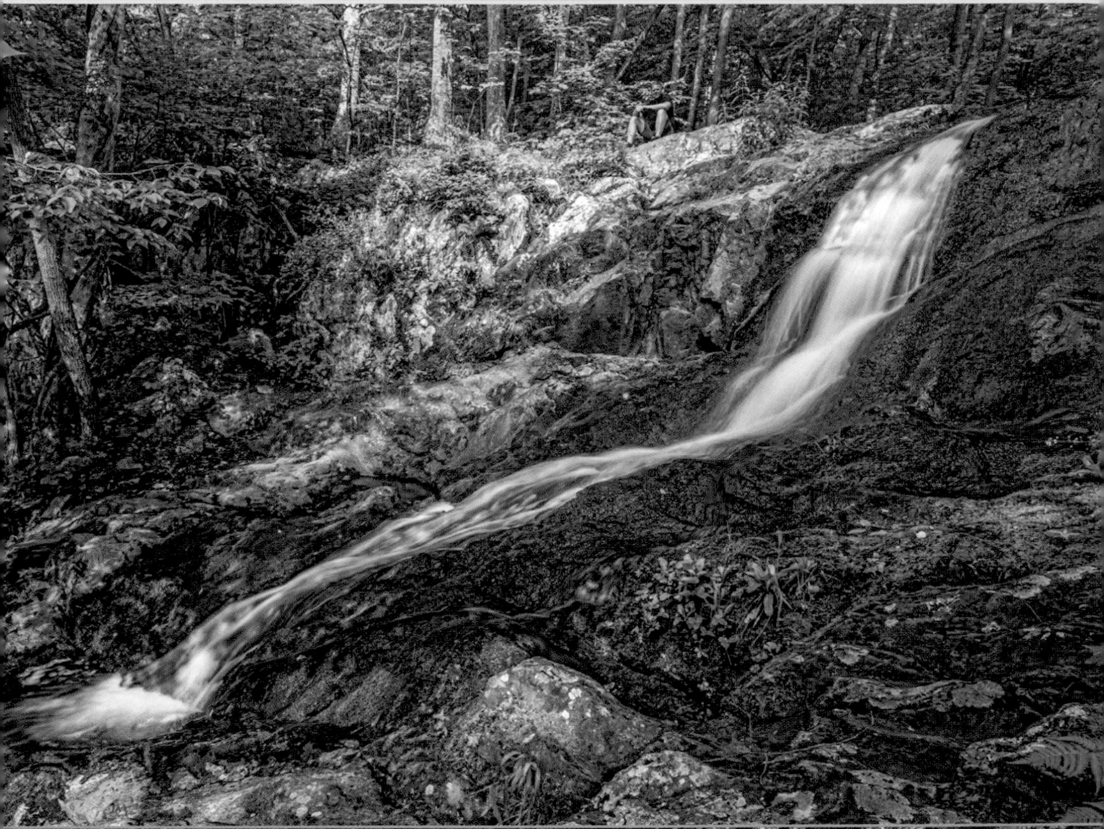

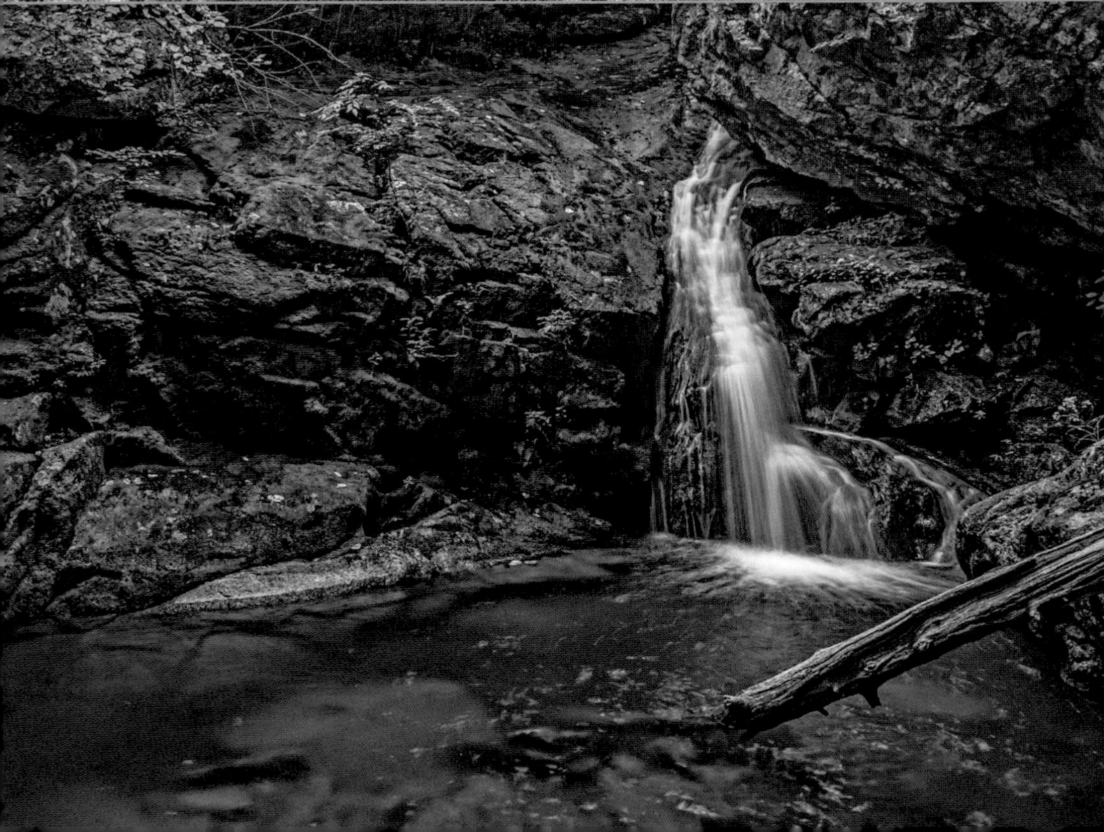

Lands Run Falls

LOCATION: North District, Shenandoah National Park

ADDRESS/GPS FOR THE FALLS: Skyline Drive; 38° 49.696′ N, 78° 11.36′ W

DIRECTIONS: Parking is at mile 9.2 on the west side of Skyline Drive.

WEBSITE: None

WATERWAY: Lands Run

HEIGHT: Three distinct drops totaling around 60 feet **CREST:** Varies

NEAREST TOWN: Front Royal

HIKE DIFFICULTY: Easy to moderate

TRAIL QUALITY: A gravel fire road to the top of the falls, and a scramble on an unofficial path to base of the falls

ROUND-TRIP DISTANCE: 1.2 miles

ADMISSION: For information on admission fees, please visit tinyurl.com/snpfees

TRIP REPORT & TIPS:

I didn't have the best light or water flow for this one, and I had to wait a bit for some slow-moving clouds to pass overhead so that I could get an acceptable image. My buddy Kevin was with me on this hike, and you should be able to see him sitting on the ledge. I figured that with as many times as I've mentioned him, he should get a cameo in the book.

The trailhead is at the beginning of a fire road that's located at the end of the parking area. This is a very straightforward and short hike and follows the fire road down to the top of the falls. User-created paths offer routes down to each of the drops; due to the conditions, I only took the time to photograph the upper drop.

Hazel Falls

LOCATION: Central District, Shenandoah National Park

ADDRESS/GPS FOR THE FALLS: Skyline Drive; 38° 38.083′ N, 78° 17.185′ W

DIRECTIONS: The Meadow Spring parking area on the east side of Skyline Drive at mile 33.5.

WEBSITE: None

WATERWAY: Hazel River

HEIGHT: 25 feet **CREST:** Varies

NEAREST TOWN: Sperryville

HIKE DIFFICULTY: Moderate, with a steep descent near the waterfall

TRAIL QUALITY: A mostly wide path, with some single-track thrown in; ranges from hard-packed dirt to rocky with exposed roots

ROUND-TRIP DISTANCE: 5.1 miles

ADMISSION: For information on admission fees, please visit tinyurl.com/snpfees

TRIP REPORT & TIPS:

This is one of my favorite hikes in Shenandoah National Park. The 5.1-mile round-trip didn't feel as long as some of the shorter but steeper hikes I'd covered, and the forest is beautiful. From the trailhead at the south end of the parking area follow the Hazel Mountain Trail (the concrete post calls it the Hazel Mountain Road). At the 0.4-mile mark, stay on the Hazel Mountain Trail, while the Buck Ridge Trail bears to the left. At the 1.6-mile mark, turn left onto the White Rocks Trail, and at the 2.4-mile mark, turn right onto the Cave and Falls Trail. Descend steeply, and when the trail levels off, follow a short distance to the falls.

Upper Rose River Falls

LOCATION: Central District, Shenandoah National Park

ADDRESS/GPS FOR THE FALLS: Skyline Drive; 38° 31.892′ N, 78° 24.524′ W

DIRECTIONS: Parking is available on the west side of Skyline Drive at the Fishers Gap Overlook parking area or a lower lot at mile 49.4.

WEBSITE: None

WATERWAY: Rose River

HEIGHT: 25 feet **CREST:** Varies

NEAREST TOWN: Elkton

HIKE DIFFICULTY: Easy, but with a 720-foot elevation gain on the steadily uphill return hike

TRAIL QUALITY: A nice, wide dirt path that becomes narrow and rocky near the waterfall

ROUND-TRIP DISTANCE: 2.5 miles

ADMISSION: For information on admission fees, please visit tinyurl.com/snpfees

TRIP REPORT & TIPS:

The Rose River Falls hike is a pleasant stroll through beautiful forest; the stream parallels the trail about halfway into the hike.

From the parking area, cross to the east side of Skyline Drive to the trailhead. Then follow the Rose River Fire Road for a very short distance, and then turn left onto the Big Meadows Horse Trail/Rose River Loop Trail. At 0.5 mile, when the Horse Trail bears to the left, continue on the Rose River Loop Trail, and at about 1.3 mile in, you'll arrive at the Upper Falls. You'll have to scramble down from the trail a short distance to reach the stream. You can continue on this trail to Dark Hollow Falls and then hike up the Rose River Fire Road back to your car. Consult a park trail map for the Rose River/Dark Hollow circuit hike.

Lower Rose River Falls

LOCATION: Central District, Shenandoah National Park

ADDRESS/GPS FOR THE FALLS: Skyline Drive; 38° 31.881′ N, 78° 24.5′ W

DIRECTIONS: Parking is available on the west side of Skyline Drive at the Fishers Gap Overlook parking area or a lower lot at mile 49.4.

WEBSITE: None

WATERWAY: Rose River

HEIGHT: 40 feet **CREST:** Varies

NEAREST TOWN: Elkton

HIKE DIFFICULTY: Easy, but with a 720-foot elevation gain on the steadily uphill return hike

TRAIL QUALITY: A nice, wide dirt path that becomes narrow and rocky near the waterfall

ROUND-TRIP DISTANCE: 2.7 miles

ADMISSION: For information on admission fees, please visit tinyurl.com/snpfees

TRIP REPORT & TIPS:

I seriously considered making the crazy scramble down to the base of the Lower Falls, but with the low water flow, and wanting to maximize my time in the park, I opted for this view from a perch off the main trail.

Follow the directions to Upper Rose River Falls (above). The perch I accessed for this image is just a few yards from the Upper Falls and on a spur path to the edge of the cliff. To access the base of the Lower Falls, look for a user-created path about 0.1 mile from the point where you scramble down to the Upper Falls.

Lewis Falls *(Lewis Spring Falls)*

LOCATION: Central District, Shenandoah National Park

ADDRESS/GPS FOR THE FALLS: Skyline Drive; 38° 31'12.95"N, 78° 26'58.18"W

DIRECTIONS: Parking is in a small lot on the west side of Skyline Drive at mile 51.4, near the Tanners Ridge Overlook.

WEBSITE: tinyurl.com/lewissnp

WATERWAY: Hawksbill Creek

HEIGHT: 80 feet **CREST:** Varies

NEAREST TOWN: Elkton

HIKE DIFFICULTY: Moderate; steep uphill return

TRAIL QUALITY: Gravel fire road at the beginning and a rocky path with exposed roots for most of the hike

ROUND-TRIP DISTANCE: 2 miles

ADMISSION: For information on admission fees, please visit tinyurl.com/snpfees

TRIP REPORT & TIPS:

Like Overall Run Falls (page 92) and South River Falls (below), Lewis Falls is another waterfall with a view. Hawksbill Creek casually flows through the forest, only to leap over the ledge into an open area that is much like an amphitheater.

From the trailhead at the north end of the parking lot on a gravel fire road, follow the gravel fire road for 0.3 mile to where you'll see an old pump house on your right. Just beyond the pump house is a trail junction; take the trail to the left. At 0.7 mile you'll reach another trail junction; stay left on the Lewis Falls Trail, and at 0.9 mile you'll arrive at the top of the falls. To reach the observation area, walk upstream a short distance, then cross the creek and follow the path to the viewing platform.

South River Falls

LOCATION: Central District, Shenandoah National Park

ADDRESS/GPS FOR THE FALLS: Skyline Drive; 38° 22.767'N, 78° 30.022'W

DIRECTIONS: Parking is near the end of the one-way route through the South River Picnic Area at mile 62.8 on Skyline Drive.

WEBSITE: www.nps.gov/shen

WATERWAY: South River

HEIGHT: 83 feet **CREST:** Varies

NEAREST TOWN: Elkton

HIKE DIFFICULTY: Moderate, with an 850-foot climb on the return hike

TRAIL QUALITY: A rocky, wide path

ROUND-TRIP DISTANCE: 2.6 miles

ADMISSION: For information on admission fees, please visit tinyurl.com/snpfees

TRIP REPORT & TIPS:

Due to low water flow and a bright sky, I only went as far as the overlook. I hope to check out the views here under better conditions. From the trailhead at the east end of the picnic area, follow the South River Trail, and at 0.1 mile you'll cross the Appalachian Trail, and then at 0.6 mile you'll get your first look at the stream. The steady descent eases here, and you'll be on more-level terrain. At 1.2 miles, cross a side stream just upstream from the overlook.

To view the falls from river level, continue past the overlook for about 250 yards, turn right onto a Forest Road and follow for about 0.5 mile to the river, then hike upstream on a narrow trail to the waterfall.

Upper Doyles River Falls

LOCATION: South District, Shenandoah National Park

ADDRESS/GPS FOR THE FALLS: Skyline Drive; 38° 14.423'N, 78° 41.406'W

DIRECTIONS: The Doyles River Parking Area is on the east side of Skyline Drive at mile 81.1.

WEBSITE: None

WATERWAY: Doyles River

HEIGHT: 28 feet **CREST:** Varies

NEAREST TOWN: Elkton

HIKE DIFFICULTY: Moderate

TRAIL QUALITY: A wide and rocky dirt path

ROUND-TRIP DISTANCE: 2.7 miles

ADMISSION: For information on admission fees, please visit tinyurl.com/snpfees

TRIP REPORT & TIPS:

My friend Kevin and I hiked the Doyles River Falls Trail during the same visit that we hiked Whiteoak Canyon and Dark Hollow Falls, which means that we caught Doyles River Falls at a perfect time. The new greens of spring brightened the surroundings, and the abundant water flow made for some terrific photos.

From the trailhead at the south end of the parking area, follow the Doyles River Trail, and at 0.7 mile you'll begin paralleling the river. At the 1-mile mark, cross a bridge over Doyles River, and at the 1.2-mile mark, you'll reach the Upper Falls. A short spur trail leads down to a stream-level view of the waterfall.

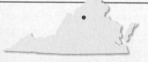

Lower Doyles River Falls

LOCATION: South District, Shenandoah National Park

ADDRESS/GPS FOR THE FALLS: Skyline Drive; 38° 14.306'N, 78° 41.479'W

DIRECTIONS: The Doyles River Parking Area is on the east side of Skyline Drive at mile 81.1.

WEBSITE: www.nps.gov/shen/doyles-river-falls.htm

WATERWAY: Doyles River

HEIGHT: 63 feet **CREST:** Varies

NEAREST TOWN: Elkton

HIKE DIFFICULTY: Moderate

TRAIL QUALITY: Narrow, steep and rocky from Upper Falls to Lower Falls

ROUND-TRIP DISTANCE: 3.2 miles

ADMISSION: For information on admission fees, please visit tinyurl.com/snpfees

TRIP REPORT & TIPS:

While the abundant water flow made for some amazing images during this particular visit to Shenandoah National Park, it hindered me a bit here at Lower Doyles River Falls. Due to the heavy spray, I was unable to get as close to the falls as I would have liked, but I was still very pleased with the images I made. The water courses every which way here, making for a dramatic waterfall and easily my favorite of the two Doyles River Falls.

From the Upper Falls (above), follow the trail downstream for 0.3 mile to the top of the Lower Falls. To reach the stream, the final 0.1 mile involves a steep and rocky descent, but it is well worthwhile.

Jones Run Falls

LOCATION: South District, Shenandoah National Park

ADDRESS/GPS FOR THE FALLS: Skyline Drive; 38° 13.784′ N, 78° 42.287′ W

DIRECTIONS: The Jones Run Parking Area is on the east side of Skyline Drive at mile 84.1.

WEBSITE: www.nps.gov/shen/doyles-river-falls.htm

WATERWAY: Jones Run

HEIGHT: 42 feet **CREST:** Varies

NEAREST TOWN: Elkton

HIKE DIFFICULTY: Moderate

TRAIL QUALITY: Wide and rocky dirt path

ROUND-TRIP DISTANCE: 3.4 miles to the top and back, and 3.7 miles to the base and back

ADMISSION: For information on admission fees, please visit tinyurl.com/snpfees

TRIP REPORT & TIPS:

I loved the fact that I could get right to the base of the falls here, and the setting is beautiful. Both sides of the falls are laden with moss and surrounded by lush greenery, giving the scene a pleasant, cool feeling. Be sure to explore downstream just a bit to take in small cascades and slides.

From the trailhead is at the south end of the small parking area follow the Jones Run Trail downhill, and in 0.1 mile you'll cross the Appalachian Trail. Then at the 0.6-mile mark, rock hop across Jones Run. The trail levels out here, making the approach to the falls a bit gentler, and at the 1.7-mile mark it reaches the top of the falls. Follow for another 0.1 mile to reach the base of the falls.

Big Branch Falls

LOCATION: South District

ADDRESS/GPS FOR THE FALLS: Sugar Hollow Road; 38° 9.97′ N, 78° 44.791′ W

DIRECTIONS: From I-64 take exit 107 near Crozet, and follow US-250 east for 1.4 miles. Turn left onto VA-240 East (Crozet Avenue), and follow for 1.4 miles. Continue straight onto VA-810, and follow for 4.4 miles to White Hall. Turn left onto VA-614 (Sugar Hollow Road), and follow for 5.5 miles to the parking area.

WEBSITE: None

WATERWAY: Big Branch

HEIGHT: 45 feet **CREST:** Varies

NEAREST TOWN: White Hall

HIKE DIFFICULTY: An easy hike with moderately difficult stream crossings in higher water

TRAIL QUALITY: Hard-packed dirt; rocky sections

ROUND-TRIP DISTANCE: 4.2 miles

ADMISSION: None

TRIP REPORT & TIPS:

You're going to have to trust me on this one—this is an actual waterfall. Big Branch is a popular swimming destination, and while the day I was there was good for swimming, it was lousy for waterfall photography.

From the trailhead, follow the gravel road for 0.5 mile to the beginning of the yellow-blazed North Fork Moormans River Trail, which parallels the stream. Reach the first stream crossing at 0.8 mile and another at 1.6 miles. At the 2-mile mark, the trail begins to get steep, and you'll notice another trail crossing the stream; stay straight and follow the yellow blazes for another 0.1 mile to the waterfall.

Falls of the Nottoway

LOCATION: Nottoway Falls Reservoir

ADDRESS/GPS FOR THE FALLS: The Falls Road; 37° 2.673′N, 78° 8′W

DIRECTIONS: From US-460 in Crewe, follow VA-49 South for about 9.3 miles, and cross a bridge over the Nottoway River. About 0.1 mile after crossing the bridge, look for a right turn onto a gravel road with a sign for a boat ramp. Follow for about 100 yards, and stay right at the fork and park near a wooden gate.

WEBSITE: tinyurl.com/nottawayva

WATERWAY: Nottoway River

HEIGHT: 30-plus feet in a series of slides

CREST: Varies

NEAREST TOWN: Victoria is a couple miles closer, but I've routed you from Crewe, due to its proximity to US-460

HIKE DIFFICULTY: Easy

TRAIL QUALITY: Dirt path

ROUND-TRIP DISTANCE: 0.4 mile

ADMISSION: None

TRIP REPORT & TIPS:

This neat series of slides on the Nottoway River is just a little over an hour from Richmond. I was met here by my good friend John Bowman, who first made me aware of this waterfall with one of his fine images of it.

From the parking area, look for a gravel service road to the right that will lead you down to the base of the VA-49 bridge spanning the river. Follow the path under the bridge and then into the woods for about 0.1 mile, then work your way down to the river.

Falls of the James

LOCATION: Richmond

ADDRESS/GPS FOR THE FALLS: T. Tyler Potterfield Memorial Bridge; 37° 32.019′N, 77° 26.672′W

DIRECTIONS: Park on 5th Street or vicinity and cross the 5th Street Pedestrian Bridge onto Brown's Island, then walk onto the T. Tyler Potterfield Memorial Bridge for the view featured here.

WEBSITE: None

WATERWAY: James River

HEIGHT: Varies **CREST:** Varies

NEAREST TOWN: Richmond

HIKE DIFFICULTY: Easy

TRAIL QUALITY: Excellent

ROUND-TRIP DISTANCE: 0.2 mile

ADMISSION: None

TRIP REPORT & TIPS:

This listing is a bit of a stretch, but bear with me. I needed one more waterfall for the Piedmont region so there would be no blank space here. I could have opted for a man-made waterfall or water spilling over a dam, but I thought you'd prefer a natural water feature. The Falls of the James actually refers to a 7-mile stretch of the James River where it drops more than 100 feet, transitioning from the piedmont to the tidewater. In this 7-mile stretch are numerous rapids and falls, both named and unnamed. Pictured here is a sunset scene of a portion of downtown Richmond captured from the T. Tyler Potterfield Memorial Bridge.

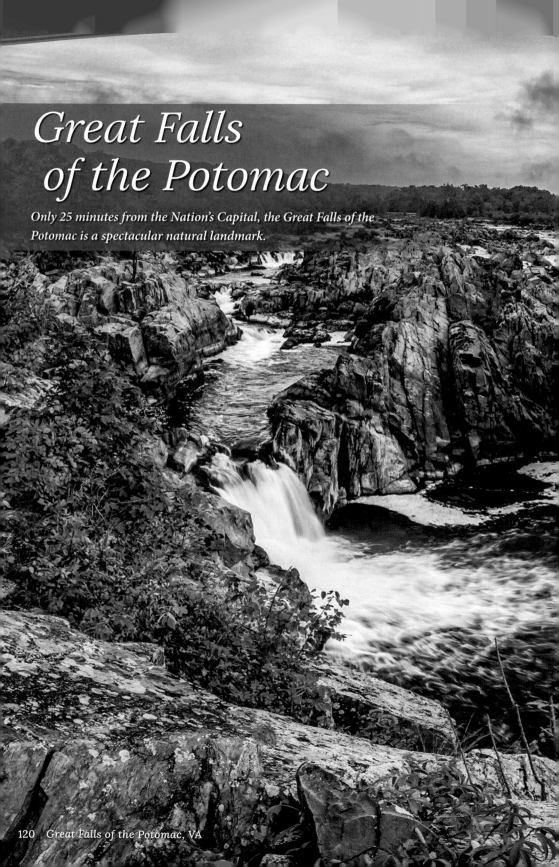

Great Falls
of the Potomac

Only 25 minutes from the Nation's Capital, the Great Falls of the Potomac is a spectacular natural landmark.

Great Falls of the Potomac

Three overlooks offer wonderful views of Great Falls, and overlooks 2 and 3 are wheelchair and stroller accessible.

LOCATION: Great Falls Park

ADDRESS/GPS FOR THE FALLS: 9200 Old Dominion Dr., McLean, VA 22102; 38° 59.802′N, 77° 15.188′W

DIRECTIONS: From Virginia via I-495, take exit 44 for VA-193 (Georgetown Pike). Turn left onto VA-193 West at the stoplight at the top of the ramp. Drive about 4 miles, and turn right onto Old Dominion Drive at the stoplight. The entrance to the park is about 1 mile down the road.

WEBSITE: nps.gov/grfa/index.htm

WATERWAY: Potomac River

HEIGHT: 40–50 feet **CREST:** Varies

NEAREST TOWN: Great Falls

HIKE DIFFICULTY: Easy

TRAIL QUALITY: Good; a wide gravel path leads from the visitor center to the three overlooks

ROUND-TRIP DISTANCE: About 0.3 mile

ADMISSION: $5 per person if entering by foot, bicycle, or horse and $10 per vehicle; consult website for fee-free days

TRIP REPORT & TIPS:

Seeing hundreds of images from Great Falls didn't prepare me for the awe-inspiring scene that spread out before me on my first visit to Great Falls. I usually take my time surveying a scene before breaking out my gear, but it took a lot longer than normal here. The vast and rugged beauty of the area just about floored me, and I wanted to take it all in slowly before getting down to business. I was there in late summer, following an extended dry spell, but even with the extremely low water flow, the sound of the water raging down below was impressive; I can't imagine the sound at high water.

I had spent the night prior to my visit with my good friend Martin Radigan and his family at their home in nearby Maryland. I followed Martin to Great Falls, and we arrived in plenty of time to hopefully catch some epic sunrise color and light. The early morning color never did materialize, but I'm more than pleased with the conditions I encountered. Martin had to head into DC for work, so he offered a few suggestions on vantage points, and left. Save for a few deer and a shy red fox, I had the place to myself for about an hour. I spent as much time as I thought I needed at the park that day, checking out the views from all three overlooks.

The more I researched Great Falls, and spoke to several of my Northern Virginia photography friends, the more I came to learn that while Great Falls is spectacularly beautiful, it's just as equally deadly. Pay close attention to the warning signs and stay well away from the water. The currents here—even on very placid-looking sections—are incredibly powerful, and deaths occur on the river every year. The visitor center and signage around the falls also warn of the dangers of falling into the water, so be careful, and stay in the designated viewing areas.

Be sure to check out Scott's Run Falls in the nearby Scott's Run Nature Preserve featured on page 124. It's only 3.5 miles away on VA-193 East/Georgetown Pike.

Scott's Run Falls

LOCATION: Scott's Run Nature Preserve

ADDRESS/GPS FOR THE FALLS: Georgetown Pike near the Swinks Mill Road intersection; 38° 58.063' N, 77° 12.164' W

DIRECTIONS: Take exit 44 off of I-495 west of Washington, DC, and follow Georgetown Pike/VA-193 west for 0.6 mile. Just beyond the intersection of Georgetown Pike and Swinks Mill Road, turn right into the parking area.

WEBSITE: tinyurl.com/vascottsrun

WATERWAY: Scott's Run

HEIGHT: 15 feet **CREST:** Varies

NEAREST TOWN: McClean

HIKE DIFFICULTY: Easy

TRAIL QUALITY: Gravel roadbed

ROUND-TRIP DISTANCE: 1.2 miles

ADMISSION: None

TRIP REPORT & TIPS:

Scott's Run Falls is in a nice wooded setting and pours over an interesting cut in the tiny gorge. With an open canopy, you'll need to arrive early in the morning or late in the afternoon on sunny days to avoid harsh light. The waters of Scott's Run empty into the mighty Potomac River just a few yards downstream from the waterfall.

From the parking area, go through the gate and follow the trail—which is a wide gravel road—to the falls. You'll cross the stream twice, but raised concrete pillars will keep your feet dry. While it's rated as an easy hike, there is a steep ascent after the second stream crossing and then a steep descent to the falls.

Piney Run Falls

LOCATION: Potomac Wayside Park

ADDRESS/GPS FOR THE FALLS: US-340; 39° 19.208' N, 77° 42.739' W

DIRECTIONS: From US-340 West in Sandy Hook, Maryland, travel less than 1 mile as you cross the Potomac River into Virginia. The park will be on your right almost immediately after crossing the bridge. Please note that if you travel east from Harpers Ferry, WV, you'll need to cross the bridge into Maryland, turn around, and come back; there are no left turns allowed into the park from the eastbound lane.

WATERWAY: Piney Run

HEIGHT: 20 feet **CREST:** Varies

NEAREST TOWN: Sandy Hook, Maryland

HIKE DIFFICULTY: Easy

TRAIL QUALITY: Dirt, with rocks and exposed roots

ROUND-TRIP DISTANCE: Around 75 yards

ADMISSION: None

TRIP REPORT & TIPS:

Like Scott's Run Falls (above), Piney Run Falls is not far from the Potomac River. It too is in a nice wooded setting, but Piney Run Falls is nestled under a thicker canopy of trees, as opposed to the more open canopy found at Scott's Run. I was fortunate to visit Piney Run Falls during a couple days of summer rainfall, allowing me to witness this beautiful waterfall with great water flow.

From the parking area right next to US-340, simply follow one of several well-worn paths down to the waterfall.

12 More Virginia Waterfalls to Explore

	GPS Coordinates	Location	Height
	Garrett Creek Falls 36° 45.432' N 82° 4.991' W	North of Abingdon on County Road 611/Garrett Creek Road. This waterfall is on private property but can be viewed from the public road.	45 feet
	Tank Hollow Falls 36° 56.408' N 82° 9.258' W	At the edge of town in Cleveland, VA, down the hill from the church on the hill on Hall Street.	60 feet
	Unnamed Falls on Tumbling Creek #1 36° 55.893' N 81° 49.842' W	Clinch Mountain Wildlife Management Area—one of several unnamed falls along this beautiful stream. See page 28 for the named falls.	6 feet
	Unnamed Falls on Tumbling Creek #2 36° 55.883' N 81° 49.877' W	Clinch Mountain Wildlife Management Area—one of several unnamed falls along this beautiful stream. See page 28 for the named falls.	10 feet
	Unnamed Falls on Tumbling Creek #3 36° 55.862' N 81° 49.912' W	Clinch Mountain Wildlife Management Area—one of several unnamed falls along this beautiful stream. See page 28 for the named falls.	A 25-foot run of cascades
	Upper Fox Creek Falls 36° 41.82' N 81° 28.011' W	About 20 yards upstream of Fox Creek Falls (page 44).	6 feet

	GPS Coordinates	Location	Height
	Upper Comers Creek Falls 36° 42.749' N 81° 28.398' W	About 25 yards from the Comers Creek Falls Trailhead (page 44).	7 feet
	Blue Suck Falls 37° 54.265' N 79° 49.233' W	Douthat State Park. Stony Run Falls is also located in the park; both are slide-type falls and need to be visited after a lot of rain.	35 feet
	Apple Orchard Bonus 37° 30.916' N 79° 31.967' W	Blue Ridge Parkway—a nice bonus to your hike to Apple Orchard Falls (page 80).	10 feet
	Hogcamp Branch Cascade 38° 31.116' N 78° 25.417' W	Shenandoah National Park, along the Dark Hollow Falls Trail (page 102).	5 feet
	Doyles River Cascade 38° 14.467' N 78° 41.35' W	Shenandoah National Park, along the Doyles River Falls Trail (page 114).	10 feet
	Hollow Brook Falls 39° 4.153' N 77° 54.179' W	Park where the A.T. crosses Morgan's Mill Road near Mount Weather. Hike north for a little under 0.9 mile to the stream, cross the creek, and follow the spur trail about 100 yards upstream to the waterfall.	15 feet

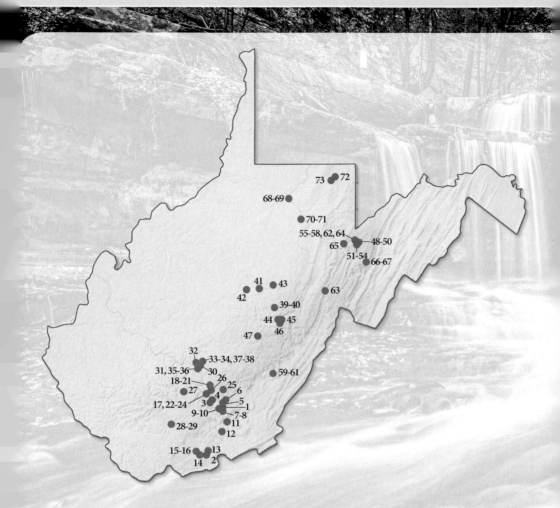

Map of West Virginia's Waterfalls

Upper New River Gorge and Bluestone River Tributaries

① Sandstone Falls (p. 130)

② Brush Creek Falls (p. 134)

③ Kate's Falls (p. 138)

④ Lower Glade Creek Falls (p. 138)

⑤ Claypool Falls (p. 140)

⑥ Harvey Falls (p. 140)

⑦ Big Branch Falls (p. 142)

⑧ Homestead Falls (p. 142)

⑨ Fall Branch Falls #1 (p. 144)

⑩ Fall Branch Falls #3 (p. 144)

⑪ Little Wolf Creek Falls (p. 146)

⑫ Pipestem Falls (p. 146)

⑬ White Oak Creek Falls (p. 148)

⑭ Wolf Creek Falls (p. 148)

⑮ Campbell Falls (p. 150)

⑯ Mash Fork Falls (p. 150)

Central New River Gorge

⑰ Dunloup Creek Falls (p. 152)

⑱ Wolf Creek Falls (p. 156)

⑲ Marr Branch Falls (p. 158)

⑳ Upper Fern Creek Falls (p. 160)

● Top 25   ● Must-See   ● Other

Sandstone Falls

An early morning visit to Sandstone Falls often results in heavy fog covering the river, while an evening visit can lead to amazing clouds and light above the falls.

Sandstone Falls, WV 131

Sandstone Falls

Sandstone Falls marks the transition zone of the New River from a wide river of large bottomlands to a narrow, rugged river raging through a deep boulder-strewn gorge.

LOCATION: New River Gorge National River

ADDRESS/GPS FOR THE FALLS: River Road; 37° 45.413′ N, 80° 54.419′ W

DIRECTIONS: From WV-20 in Hinton, follow New River Road for about 8 miles to the Sandstone Falls Day Use Area.

WEBSITE: tinyurl.com/sandstonewv

WATERWAY: New River

HEIGHT: 10–25 feet (the river is divided by a series of islands) **CREST:** 1,500 feet

NEAREST TOWN: Hinton

HIKE DIFFICULTY: Easy to Moderate

TRAIL QUALITY: Boardwalk and metal footbridge; off-trail it is rocky with exposed roots

ROUND-TRIP DISTANCE: The boardwalk distance is just under 0.5 mile

ADMISSION: None

TRIP REPORT & TIPS:

Sandstone Falls is one of my favorite waterfalls in West Virginia, and it is easy to access, thanks to an elaborate 0.25-mile-long boardwalk and bridge system. The first bridge is a small one that crosses a man-made channel that once diverted water for a grist mill used by local farmers. The boardwalk leads to an overlook of the lower section of falls, which has about a 10-foot drop. To the left of the boardwalk you'll notice the Island Loop Trail, which leads you through the Appalachian Riverside Flat Rock Plant Community, a unique botanical ecosystem in West Virginia. The second bridge crosses a wide natural channel that offers nice views of the lower section of falls in the distance. The boardwalk ends at an overlook with views of a 20- to 25-foot section of the falls.

Here is where I invite you to leave the boardwalk and explore! Just a few feet before the boardwalk ends, look for a trail to the right. The trail leads you to closer views of the lower falls, but also, after a few stream crossings, leads you to an island with magnificent views of the river and the main section of falls. To reach the island, follow the trail to the first stream crossing and, shortly thereafter, another smaller stream crossing. Then, bear to the left a little and follow the well-worn path as it leads toward the river and then one final stream crossing. Work your way through a couple large boulders, bear to the right and scramble up the exposed bedrock, and then bear to the left toward the roar of the falls. After a few yards, prepare to be stopped in your tracks and mesmerized by the view in front of you! I don't know enough adjectives to describe it properly, just know that you'll be hooked, just like I was many years ago.

Note: There will be times where the river is running high and the stream crossings could be a dangerous undertaking.

Lastly, on your way to Sandstone Falls, you'll pass two outstanding sources for waterfalls. Big Branch (page 142) and Fall Branch (page 144) are wonderful streams with beautiful cascades and waterfalls. Time your visit when there's ample water flow so you can fully take advantage of what these two streams have to offer.

Brush Creek Falls

You're going to love this one! So many great vantage points to choose from, and a wonderful opportunity to use your telephoto lenses to isolate individual sections of the waterfall.

Brush Creek Falls

Adjacent to Brush Creek Falls is the Nature Conservancy's Brush Creek Preserve, a great place to see beautiful spring wildflowers, migrating warblers, and dramatic limestone and sandstone cliffs.

LOCATION: Near I-77 in Mercer County off of Brush Creek Falls Road

ADDRESS/GPS FOR THE FALLS: Brush Creek Falls Road; 37° 27.995′N, 81° 3.635′W

DIRECTIONS: From I-77, take exit 14 and travel east for 0.1 mile. Turn left onto Eads Mill Road, and follow for 3.3 miles, then turn right onto Brush Creek Falls Road. Follow for 0.3 mile, and the parking area is on the left, just after crossing Brush Creek. The trail begins at the small picnic shelter.

WEBSITE: tinyurl.com/wvbrushcreek

WATERWAY: Brush Creek

HEIGHT: 33 feet **CREST:** Varies

NEAREST TOWN: Athens

HIKE DIFFICULTY: Easy

TRAIL QUALITY: A wide, rocky dirt path

ROUND-TRIP DISTANCE: 0.5 mile

ADMISSION: None

TRIP REPORT & TIPS:

My first visit to this impressive waterfall was over 30 years ago, and after countless visits, Brush Creek Falls remains one of my favorites. Your first view of the falls will actually be what I call the Upper Falls—a series of small cascades that makes up the ledge of Brush Creek Falls. After photographing the upper section of the falls, continue down the trail a short distance past a wooden fence and make an abrupt switchback to the left and down to the creek.

Several nice vantage points for photographing Brush Creek Falls can be found once you descend the path from the upper trail. The pool is rather large, though, so my favorite vantage points are actually in the creek itself, or from the other side of the creek.

Note: Be careful if you decide to wade into and/or across the creek; all stream crossings should be made with extra caution due to slick rocks and turbulent water.

From the parking area, the trail begins slightly uphill from the picnic shelter, and follows an easy but rocky path to the falls. Grist and woolen mills were on this site in the mid 1800s, and the trail was once a narrow-gauge railroad used by the Bluestone Land and Lumber Company to haul logs out of the canyon. Notice the remnants of the mill on the far side of the stream, near the top of the waterfall.

For additional photo opportunities, there are some very nice stream scenes and small cascades downstream from Brush Creek Falls; accessing them will require some creek walking, or steep scrambles down from the trail. Lastly, one more neat little cascade is on the other side of the road at the parking area; you can't miss it.

When Brush Creek is raging and you have the time, you should hike on down the trail to White Oak Creek Falls (page 148). It needs a lot of rain to make the hike worthwhile, but it's a beauty and shouldn't be missed when the conditions warrant a visit.

Kate's Falls

LOCATION: New River Gorge National River

ADDRESS/GPS FOR THE FALLS: Glade Creek Trail; 37° 46.517' N, 81° 1.9' W

DIRECTIONS: Note: The following description is for the Upper Glade Creek Trailhead and is only for high-clearance/4 WD vehicles. The Lower Glade Creek Falls (below) listing provides alternate directions to this waterfall via a longer route. From Beckley, take I-64 East 4.5 miles, then take the Shady Spring exit (exit 129A), and follow south on WV-9. Travel 0.5 mile toward Little Beaver State Park (turning left at the junction with WV-307 after 0.3 mile). Turn left onto Scott Branch Road (just before Fire Tower Road). Follow this road down to Glade Creek (about 1 mile). Cross the bridge for trailhead parking.

WEBSITE: tinyurl.com/gladecreekwv

WATERWAY: Kates Branch

HEIGHT: 25 feet **CREST:** Varies

NEAREST TOWN: Shady Spring

HIKE DIFFICULTY: Easy

TRAIL QUALITY: A wide, gravel path

ROUND-TRIP DISTANCE: 2.4 miles

ADMISSION: None

TRIP REPORT & TIPS:

Kate's Falls is another personal favorite of mine, but it needs a lot of rain to really shine.

From the parking area, follow the Glade Creek trail—a former narrow-gauge railbed—downstream for about 1 mile, then look for the Kate's Falls Spur Trail on the right. Follow it for 0.2 mile up a some-what steep and rocky path.

Lower Glade Creek Falls

LOCATION: New River Gorge National River

ADDRESS/GPS FOR THE FALLS: Glade Creek Trail; 37° 48.948' N, 81° 0.506' W

DIRECTIONS: From Fayetteville, follow US-19 South for about 10 miles to Glen Jean, and turn left at the stop light. Turn right onto WV-61 South and follow for 2.8 miles. Turn left, staying on WV-61, and follow for another 4.6 miles. Turn left onto WV-41 North, and follow for 4 miles toward Prince. Turn right onto the Glade Creek Road, just before the bridge at Prince. Follow the gravel road 6 miles to the Glade Creek Trailhead.

WEBSITE: tinyurl.com/gladecreekwv

WATERWAY: Glade Creek

HEIGHT: 12 feet **CREST:** Varies

NEAREST TOWN: Prince

HIKE DIFFICULTY: Easy

TRAIL QUALITY: Mostly wide, with some areas of single-track; dirt path with areas of rocks and exposed roots

ROUND-TRIP DISTANCE: 1.8 miles

ADMISSION: None

TRIP REPORT & TIPS:

I always enjoy the easy hike to Lower Glade Creek Falls, especially during the spring when I'm rewarded with wildflow-ers along the entire length of the hike.

From the parking area, follow the Glade Creek Trail upstream for almost 1 mile. You can make some decent photographs from the trail, but I'd recommend scrambling down an unofficial spur path to the creek to explore other vantage points.

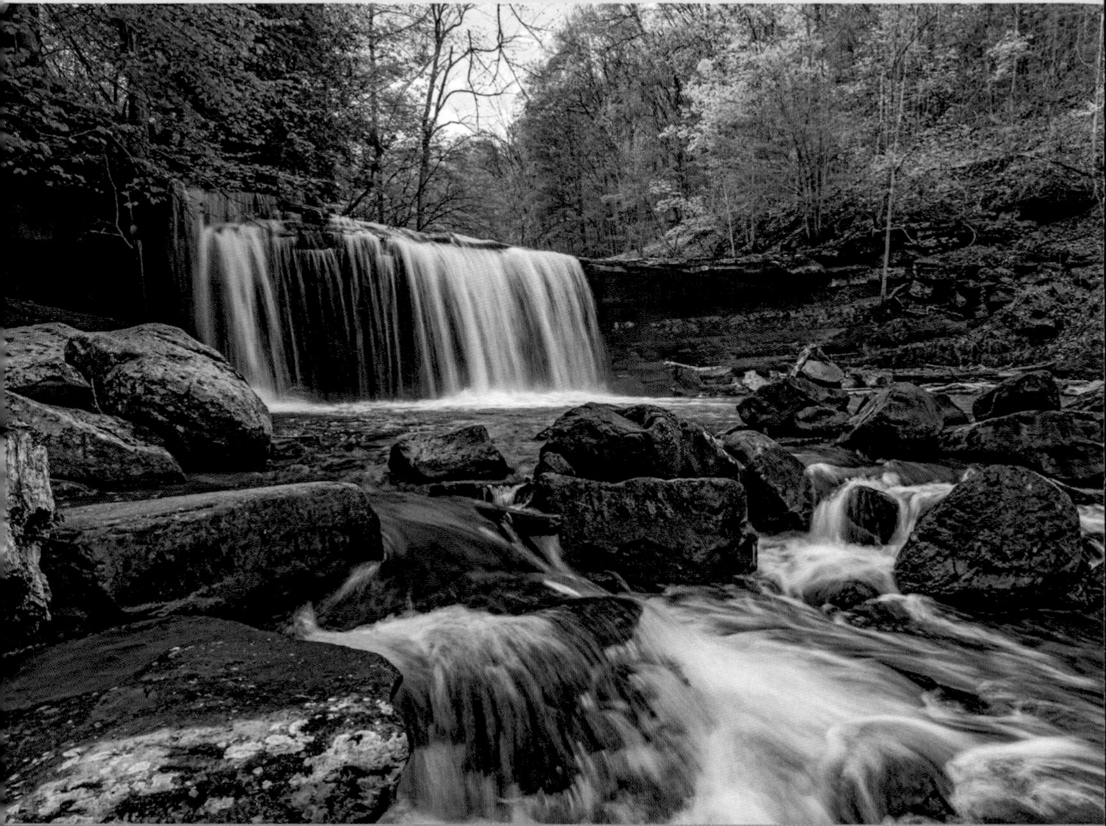

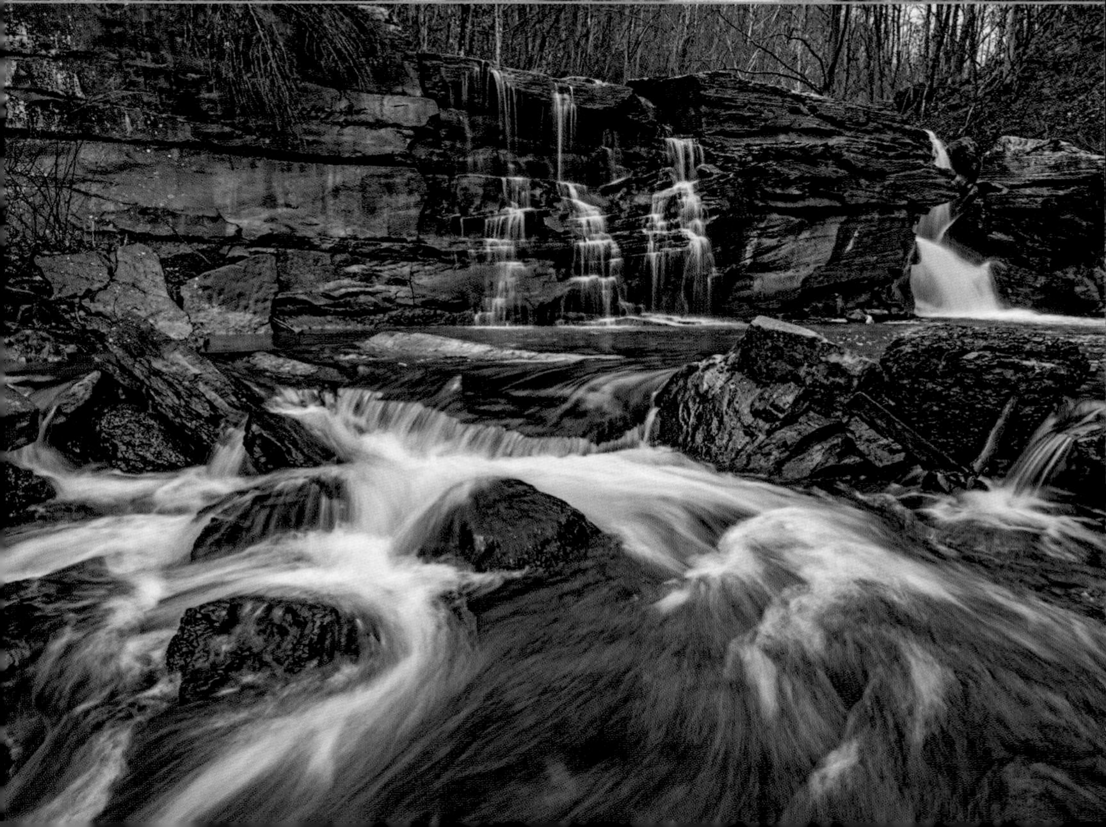

Claypool Falls

LOCATION: New River Gorge National River

ADDRESS/GPS FOR THE FALLS: Claypool Road; 37°49'24.98" N, 80° 54.349' W

DIRECTIONS: From I-64, take the Sandstone exit (exit 139), and turn right onto Meadow Creek Road. Follow for a little under 3 miles to the town of Meadow Creek, and at a church in a sharp left turn, stay straight onto Claypool Road. Follow for about 1.5 miles, and look for a pullout on the right just before the waterfall.

WEBSITE: None

WATERWAY: Meadow Creek

HEIGHT: 20 feet **CREST:** Varies

NEAREST TOWN: Meadow Creek

HIKE DIFFICULTY: Roadside view or short scramble down to creek

TRAIL QUALITY: Roadside view or short, steep scramble on dirt path

ROUND-TRIP DISTANCE: Roadside

ADMISSION: None

TRIP REPORT & TIPS:

Access down to the waterfall requires a short, but steep, descent that will place you rather close to the falls. This is your typical shelf fall with a large pool, so I prefer the longer views from downstream, so I can include the rock-strewn stream in the foreground. There are some nice cascades just upstream of the waterfall, so be sure to take a look. For those of you that don't mind a little bit of adventure and stream crossings, drive on up the road a couple miles to Harvey Falls (below).

Harvey Falls

LOCATION: Upstream from Claypool Falls

ADDRESS/GPS FOR THE FALLS: Claypool Road; 37° 50.113' N, 80° 52.19' W

DIRECTIONS: From I-64, take the Sandstone exit (exit 139), and turn right onto Meadow Creek Road. Follow for a little under 3 miles to the town of Meadow Creek, and at a church in a sharp left turn, stay straight onto Claypool Road. Follow Claypool Road for around 4 miles; just after crossing Meadow Creek on a small bridge, park at a wide spot in the road on the left.

WEBSITE: None

WATERWAY: Meadow Creek

HEIGHT: 20 feet **CREST:** Varies

NEAREST TOWN: Meadow Bridge

HIKE DIFFICULTY: Moderate, due to stream crossings

TRAIL QUALITY: None; bushwhacking

ROUND-TRIP DISTANCE: 0.4 mile

ADMISSION: None

TRIP REPORT & TIPS:

I've dubbed this waterfall Harvey Falls, due to my good friend Art Harvey leading me to it. We had both heard of another waterfall upstream from Claypool Falls (page 140), and I'm glad Art found this one. When I saw Art's photos, I knew I had to see this one for myself, knowing it'd be a great addition to this book.

There is no established trail, and it's a bit of a bushwhack, but just follow Meadow Creek upstream; in about 0.2 mile you'll be at the waterfall. Be advised that a couple stream crossings are necessary, and the rocks in and along the creek can be slick.

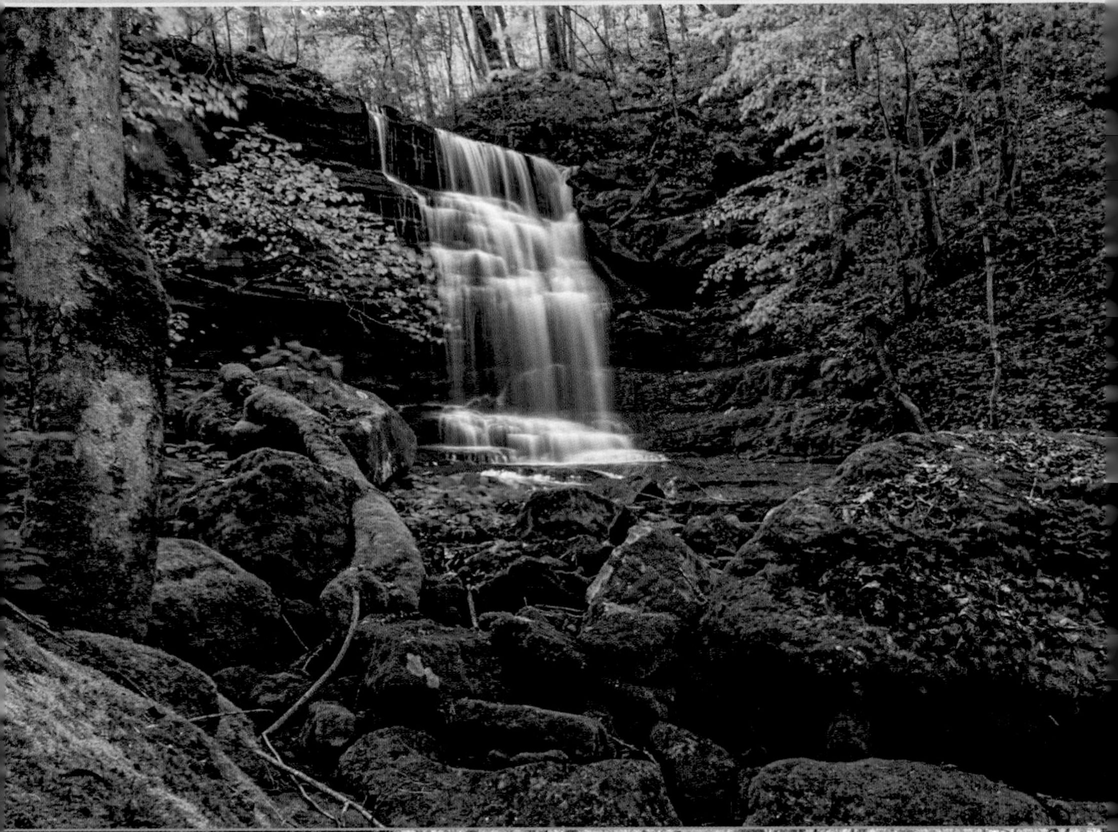

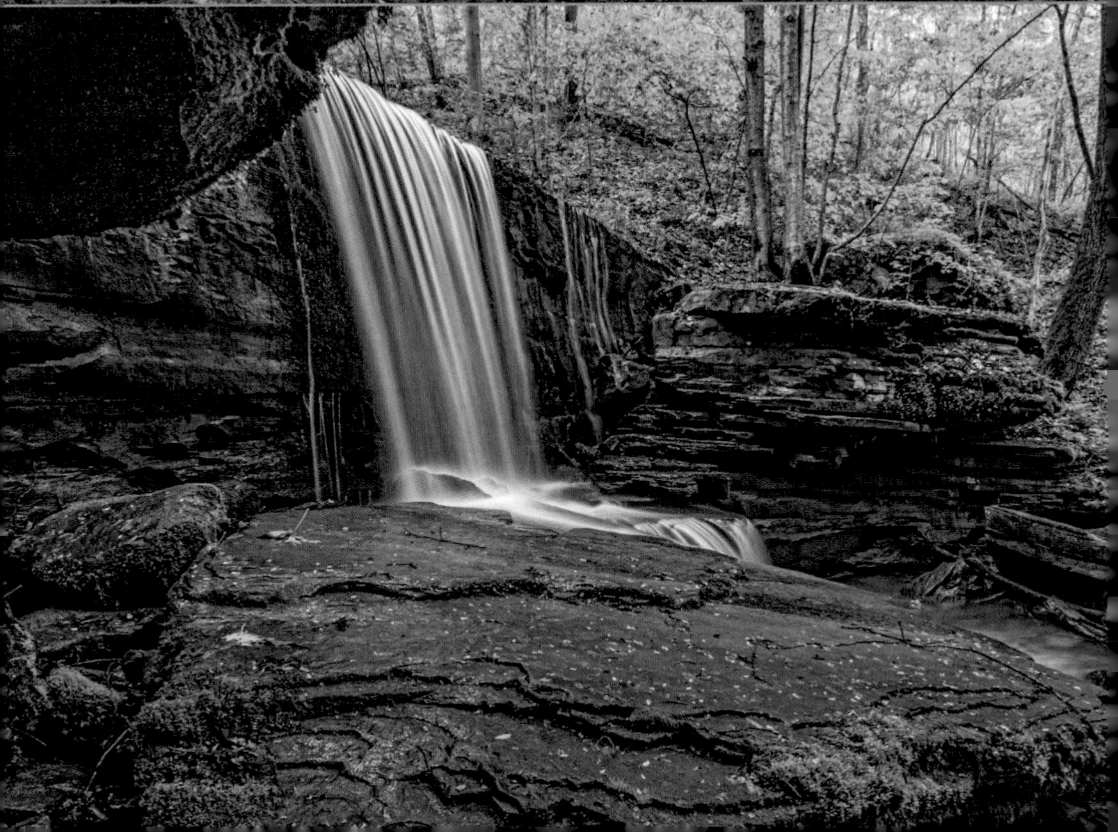

Big Branch Falls

LOCATION: New River Gorge National River

ADDRESS/GPS FOR THE FALLS: New River Road; 37° 42.824′ N, 80° 54.116′ W

DIRECTIONS: From WV-20 in Hinton, follow New River Road 4 miles to the Brooks Falls Day-Use Area on the right. The trailhead is across the road.

WEBSITE: tinyurl.com/bigbranchwv

WATERWAY: Big Branch

HEIGHT: 25 feet **CREST:** Varies

NEAREST TOWN: Hinton

HIKE DIFFICULTY: Moderate

TRAIL QUALITY: Mostly single-track, with rocks and exposed roots

ROUND-TRIP DISTANCE: 2 miles

ADMISSION: None

TRIP REPORT & TIPS:

If Big Branch were a larger watershed, the waterfalls here collectively would have received top billing. But it's a small watershed, and so it should only be visited in the spring or after periods of heavy rain. Although there are five waterfalls on Big Branch, I'm only featuring the upper two due to their individual beauty and height. Cross the road to the Big Branch trailhead, which is a 2-mile loop trail. Bear left to reach the waterfalls first. After a short distance and a stream crossing, you'll reach a junction in the trail; bear right and follow the trail uphill. At around the 1-mile mark, you'll reach Big Branch Falls, the tallest waterfall on Big Branch. To get down to the waterfall, follow a steep spur trail down into the canyon.

Homestead Falls

LOCATION: New River Gorge National River

ADDRESS/GPS FOR THE FALLS: New River Road; 37° 42.827′ N, 80° 54.21′ W

DIRECTIONS: From WV-20 in Hinton, follow New River Road 4 miles to the Brooks Falls Day Use Area on the right. The trailhead is across the road.

WEBSITE: tinyurl.com/bigbranchwv

WATERWAY: Big Branch

HEIGHT: 20 feet **CREST:** Varies

NEAREST TOWN: Hinton

HIKE DIFFICULTY: Moderate

TRAIL QUALITY: Mostly single-track, with rocks and exposed roots

ROUND-TRIP DISTANCE: 2 miles

ADMISSION: None

TRIP REPORT & TIPS:

The final waterfall on Big Branch is about 0.1 mile on up the trail from Big Branch Falls, not far from an old homestead. You'll need to scramble down from the trail for the best vantage points. From here, continue on the loop back to the trailhead, or backtrack and view the waterfalls one more time. This is one of my favorite waterfall trails in the gorge, but I encourage you to check it out in early to midspring; it's a small watershed, so more often than not, the water flow is quite low other times of the year.

Fall Branch Falls #1

LOCATION: New River Gorge National River

ADDRESS/GPS FOR THE FALLS: New River Road, Hinton, WV; 37° 44.928′ N, 80° 55.83′ W

DIRECTIONS: From WV-20 in Hinton, follow New River Road for 7 miles, and after crossing a small bridge over Fall Branch, park on either side of the road, being careful not to block any gates or driveways.

WEBSITE: None

WATERWAY: Fall Branch

HEIGHT: 6 feet **CREST:** Varies

NEAREST TOWN: Hinton

HIKE DIFFICULTY: Easy to moderate, with some stream crossings

TRAIL QUALITY: Wide and rocky for the most part

ROUND-TRIP DISTANCE: 0.6 mile

ADMISSION: None

TRIP REPORT & TIPS:

This is my favorite waterfall hike in the New River Gorge region. It's an easy hike with beautiful stream scenes, cascades, waterfalls, and wildflowers at every turn. I'm only featuring two waterfalls here, but there are at least a dozen on Fall Branch and tributary streams. It's a very small watershed, so visit in the spring or after a period of heavy rain.

The trail begins by the road and is marked by a couple boulders and easy to find. Reaching Fall Branch Falls takes a walk of a little over a 0.3 mile. The shelf is actually quite wide and continues out of frame for 10 feet or more. To reach the base of the falls from the trail, simply slide down the bank a few yards downstream.

Fall Branch Falls #3

LOCATION: New River Gorge National River

ADDRESS/GPS FOR THE FALLS: New River Road; 37° 44.829′ N, 80° 56.316′ W

DIRECTIONS: From WV-20 in Hinton, follow New River Road 7 miles, and after crossing a small bridge over Fall Branch, park on either side of the road, being careful not to block any gates or driveways.

WEBSITE: None

WATERWAY: Fall Branch

HEIGHT: 15 feet **CREST:** Varies

NEAREST TOWN: Hinton

HIKE DIFFICULTY: Easy to moderate, with some stream crossings

TRAIL QUALITY: Wide and rocky for the most part

ROUND-TRIP DISTANCE: 2 miles

TRIP REPORT & TIPS:

From Fall Branch Falls (above), continue following the trail upstream for a little over 100 yards to the first stream crossing; in 75 yards, you'll need to cross the stream again. You'll pass a small waterfall and several small cascades along the way to the third waterfall, featured here. At the 0.9-mile mark, the trail begins a slight ascent, and although not totally necessary, I suggest crossing the stream here as it makes accessing the waterfall a bit easier. Once you cross the stream, you'll be on another old road, but this one is very much overgrown. Continue upstream for a short distance, and about 10 yards from the waterfall, look for the obvious passage down to the stream.

Little Wolf Creek Falls

LOCATION: Little Wolf Creek Road

ADDRESS/GPS FOR THE FALLS: Little Wolf Creek Road; 37° 36.25' N, 80° 49.05' W

DIRECTIONS: From Hinton, follow WV-3 South for about 5 miles to the junction with WV-12. Continue straight on WV-12 for around 3.2 miles, and look for a right turn onto Little Wolf Creek Road. Follow for about 0.7 mile, and look for a pulloff to the left as you're driving uphill. Park here; Little Wolf Creek Falls is down below.

WEBSITE: None

WATERWAY: Little Wolf Creek

HEIGHT: 15 feet **CREST:** Varies

NEAREST TOWN: Hinton

HIKE DIFFICULTY: Easy short, but steep, walk down to the falls

TRAIL QUALITY: Dirt path

ROUND-TRIP DISTANCE: 50 yards

ADMISSION: None

TRIP REPORT & TIPS:

I could dub this one Harvey Falls Part II, because it's another one my good friend Art Harvey found and took me to. The well-worn path down to the creek makes it obvious that this waterfall is well known, at least by the locals. But after chasing West Virginia waterfalls for 20-plus years, it's one that escaped me. It just shows how many more waterfalls are out there for us to find! It's easy to get to this one, just follow the obvious path down to the waterfall and have fun! While not listed in the book, there is another waterfall about a half mile up the road that is worth checking out as well.

Pipestem Falls

LOCATION: Pipestem Falls Park

ADDRESS/GPS FOR THE FALLS: WV-20; 37° 32.868' N, 80° 57.57' W

DIRECTIONS: Pipestem Falls is located 2.7 miles north of Pipestem Resort State Park on WV-20— park in an obvious pulloff near a large grassy area.

WEBSITE: None

WATERWAY: Pipestem Creek

HEIGHT: 30 feet **CREST:** Varies

NEAREST TOWN: Pipestem

HIKE DIFFICULTY: Roadside view, or a moderate scramble to the base

TRAIL QUALITY: Steep and rocky dirt path down to the falls

ROUND-TRIP DISTANCE: Roadside

ADMISSION: None

TRIP REPORT & TIPS:

For years, the only way to see Pipestem Falls was to scramble down to the creek below the falls. Thankfully, today, after a lot of work, you can get a nice view of a large portion of the falls from near the parking area. However, if you're up for it, you should make the steep scramble on an unofficial path down to the creek for the best views of this beautiful waterfall.

Be sure to check out the section of the creek just upstream of the falls. You'll find a pretty little waterfall there too.

White Oak Creek Falls

LOCATION: Brush Creek Preserve

ADDRESS/GPS FOR THE FALLS: About 1.75 miles from Brush Creek Falls (page 134); 37° 28.695′ N, 81° 2.968′ W

DIRECTIONS: From I-77, take exit 14 and travel east for 0.1 mile. Turn left onto Eads Mill Road, and follow for 3.3 miles to Brush Creek Falls Road on the right. Follow for 0.3 mile, and the parking area is on the left, just after crossing Brush Creek. The trail begins at the small picnic shelter.

WEBSITE: None

WATERWAY: White Oak Creek

HEIGHT: 40 feet **CREST:** Varies

NEAREST TOWN: Athens

HIKE DIFFICULTY: Easy hike, but a difficult climb up to the falls

TRAIL QUALITY: Fairly wide dirt path, with some areas of rocks and exposed roots

ROUND-TRIP DISTANCE: 3.8 miles

ADMISSION: None

TRIP REPORT & TIPS:

This is great addition to your Brush Creek Falls hike (page 134) if the water level is high enough.

The trail begins at the parking area. Follow for about 1.9 miles, passing Brush Creek Falls at the 0.25-mile mark. You'll encounter Whiteoak Creek where it empties into the Bluestone River, and while you can catch a glimpse of the falls from here, you'll need to do some serious scrambling up to the waterfall to view it in all its glory.

Note: If you decide to make the journey up to the waterfall, do so with care, as you'll be on loose shale and on a slippery slope.

Wolf Creek Falls

LOCATION: Roadside—Route 20 near Camp Creek

ADDRESS/GPS FOR THE FALLS: Route 20; 37° 28.316′ N, 81° 6.618′ W

DIRECTIONS: From I-77, take the Camp Creek exit (exit 20), and follow US-19 South toward Spanishburg. Travel 3.6 miles, and after crossing a bridge over Wolf Creek, look for a pulloff on the left with room for a few cars.

WEBSITE: None

WATERWAY: Wolf Creek

HEIGHT: 25 feet **CREST:** Varies

NEAREST TOWN: Spanishburg

HIKE DIFFICULTY: Roadside view, or a steep scramble down to the waterfall

TRAIL QUALITY: Roadside view, or a slippery, steep scramble

ROUND-TRIP DISTANCE: Roadside view, or 20 yards down to the falls and back

ADMISSION: None

TRIP REPORT & TIPS:

Wolf Creek is a tributary of the Bluestone River, and although it's a roadside waterfall, Wolf Creek Falls is below the road and somewhat out of sight. The roadside view is OK, but a steep scramble down to the creek is encouraged if you really want to take in its beauty. I suggest having a long length of rope with you, so that you can tie off on the guardrail and have some support on the scramble down to the creek. You can combine your visit to this falls with the two waterfalls (page 150) at Camp Creek State Park.

Campbell Falls

LOCATION: Camp Creek State Park and Forest

ADDRESS/GPS FOR THE FALLS: 2390 County Highway 19/5, Camp Creek, WV 25820; 37° 31.059' N, 81° 7.749' W

DIRECTIONS: From I-77, take exit 20, turn right, and follow for 0.1 mile if coming from southbound I-77 or 0.3 mile if coming from northbound I-77. Turn right onto Camp Creek Road, and enter the park at 1.8 miles. After 2.5 miles, in a traffic circle, bear right, then continue straight on the gravel road through the Blue Jay Campground. Park in the designated area near the gate.

WEBSITE: tinyurl.com/campcreekwv

WATERWAY: Camp Creek

HEIGHT: 15 feet **CREST:** Varies

NEAREST TOWN: Athens

HIKE DIFFICULTY: Easy

TRAIL QUALITY: Gravel road

ROUND-TRIP DISTANCE: 0.5 mile

ADMISSION: None

TRIP REPORT & TIPS:

Campbell Falls is where I cut my teeth on waterfall photography. I spent countless hours honing my skills here. To this day, it's still one of my favorite places, especially during the spring, when the new greens are exploding around the falls. Numerous vantage points are available here, and be sure to check out a unique, angled creek-wide shelf cascade about 0.25 mile upstream.

The trail to Campbell Falls is actually the gravel road leading to the Double C Campground in Camp Creek State Park. From the designated parking area, follow the road 0.25 mile to the waterfall.

Mash Fork Falls

LOCATION: Camp Creek State Park and Forest

ADDRESS/GPS FOR THE FALLS: 2390 County Highway 19/5, Camp Creek, WV 25820; 37° 30.046' N, 81° 8.546' W

DIRECTIONS: From I-77, take exit 20, turn right, and follow for 0.1 mile if coming from southbound I-77 or 0.3 mile if coming from northbound I-77. Turn right onto Camp Creek Road and enter the park at 1.8 miles, and at 2.2 miles, turn left at the playground area. Follow this road 0.2 mile, and bear right onto a gravel road, and follow for 0.3 mile.

WEBSITE: tinyurl.com/campcreekwv

WATERWAY: Mash Fork

HEIGHT: 7 feet **CREST:** Varies

NEAREST TOWN: Athens

HIKE DIFFICULTY: Roadside View

TRAIL QUALITY: Good

ROUND-TRIP DISTANCE: Roadside

ADMISSION: None

TRIP REPORT & TIPS:

Just drive right up to this beautiful little waterfall, and be prepared to spend a lot of time exploring all the photography options here. My favorite compositions are from in the creek itself, with the cascading water rushing through the scene. Another favorite vantage point here is on the left bank, perched on a ledge just above the falls. Mash Fork Falls is in a small watershed, so in the drier months it is often just a trickle, but when the stream is flowing at full force, Mash Fork Falls is nothing short of spectacular.

Dunloup Creek Falls

Consistent water levels in even the driest of summer months make this a wonderful four-season waterfall.

Dunloup Creek Falls, WV   153

Dunloup Creek Falls

Dunloup Creek Falls is always a favorite among my photography workshop participants.

LOCATION: New River Gorge National River

ADDRESS/GPS FOR THE FALLS: County Road 25/Thurmond Road; 37° 56.291′N, 81° 5.845′W

DIRECTIONS: From US-19 South in Glen Jean, turn left at the stoplight (watch for New River Gorge National River signs), then left again onto WV-16/WV-61 North. Follow for 0.5 mile, then turn right, cross the bridge, and at the bank, turn left and follow toward the historic railroad town of Thurmond. Dunloup Creek will soon parallel County Road 25/Thurmond Road, and at 4.8 miles, look for a pullout on the right.

WEBSITE: None

WATERWAY: Dunloup Creek

HEIGHT: 20 feet **CREST:** Varies

NEAREST TOWN: Glen Jean

HIKE DIFFICULTY: Roadside view, or a short scramble down to the creek

TRAIL QUALITY: Roadside view; if you opt to hike, it's a scramble down a steep, rocky path with exposed roots

ROUND-TRIP DISTANCE: Roadside view, or 20 yards

ADMISSION: None

TRIP REPORT & TIPS:

I love to get my feet wet at this waterfall. From the center of the stream or from the far bank, Dunloup Creek Falls takes on an entirely different look. Plus, it's just so neat to capture the cascading water rushing through the frame.

The roadside pullout offers a nice view from above, but even if you don't want to get in the creek, you should still make the short, but steep, scramble to take in the full beauty of this waterfall. Be careful along the ledge at the bottom, as overspray from the waterfall makes it pretty slick. And if there's a lot of falling water, getting into the creek is not an option. Be satisfied with the vantage points from along the bank.

Another nice vantage point is from a small outcropping above the waterfall; here you can use a tree branch arching over the stream to frame the scene. Be sure to spend some time exploring the creek upstream and downstream from the waterfall, as there are numerous small cascades and beautiful stream scenes available. One small cascade I am particularly fond of is a couple hundred yards upstream. And don't miss a waterfall I've dubbed "Little Brother," listed on page 170; this little guy is so much fun to shoot.

Wolf Creek Falls

LOCATION: New River Gorge National River

ADDRESS/GPS FOR THE FALLS: Fayette Station Road; 38° 3.624'N, 81° 4.838'W

DIRECTIONS: From the New River Gorge Bridge Visitors Center in Lansing, follow Fayette Station Road down to the river, cross the New River, and continue on Fayette Station Road up the mountain. In a sharp switchback, there's a parking area for the Kaymoor Trail. The waterfall access is about 30 yards back down the road.

WEBSITE: None

WATERWAY: Wolf Creek

HEIGHT: 20 feet **CREST:** Varies

NEAREST TOWN: Fayetteville

HIKE DIFFICULTY: Strenuous

TRAIL QUALITY: Poor

ROUND-TRIP DISTANCE: A steep roadside scramble of 50–75 feet

ADMISSION: None

TRIP REPORT & TIPS:

While this is a roadside waterfall, many folks driving by miss out on Wolf Creek Falls. It's hidden deep in the canyon and especially difficult to spot when the trees are full of leaves. Wolf Creek is a special waterfall to me; it's the second New River Gorge waterfall I photographed, with my first visit here over 20 years ago. Park at the Kaymoor Trail and backtrack down the road about 30 yards, and you'll see an informal path. This path is very steep, and I think of the descent as more of a controlled fall, as you make your way steeply down into the canyon. About halfway down you'll encounter a jungle of rhododendron, and although you have to duck a little as you go through, you'll be thankful for the lending hand the branches afford. Once through the thicket, you'll be at the base of the falls. There aren't tons of vantage points here; my favorite spot to photograph Wolf Creek Falls is from a small ledge very near where you leave the rhododendron jungle. I've also crossed the creek and photographed from the opposite bank and from a bit downstream of the falls. There's another neat vantage point on a ledge above the waterfall.

Marr Branch Falls

LOCATION: New River Gorge National River

ADDRESS/GPS FOR THE FALLS: Fayette Station Road; 38° 4.478′ N, 81° 5.573′ W

DIRECTIONS: On US-19, turn onto Fayette Station Road, which is south of the New River Gorge Bridge. Follow it a little over 1 mile, and park on the left near a small bridge over Marr Branch. Fayette Station Road becomes one-way here, so you'll need to leave the road because you're going the wrong way beyond this point.

WEBSITE: None

WATERWAY: Marr Branch

HEIGHT: 30 feet **CREST:** Varies

NEAREST TOWN: Fayetteville

HIKE DIFFICULTY: Moderate to strenuous

TRAIL QUALITY: An unofficial dirt path that's narrow, steep, and rocky

ROUND-TRIP DISTANCE: 0.4 mile

ADMISSION: None

TRIP REPORT & TIPS:

Much like Wolf Creek Falls (page 156), many folks miss this roadside waterfall. They'll easily spot the much smaller Upper Marr Branch Falls (page 160), with no idea that this hidden beauty exists. Marr Branch Falls isn't as deep into the canyon as Wolf Creek, but it is hard to see as you're driving by. There are two options for accessing the beautiful and rugged Marr Branch Falls. The quickest, but most difficult option—especially due to a recent rockslide—is to simply look for an obvious path down from the road, follow it downstream a very short distance, and watch for a jumble of boulders and large rocks. Carefully work your way down to the base of Marr Branch Falls here. The somewhat easier option is to make your way down the path from the road, but instead of working your way downstream, continue down the path to the creek. Spend a little time shooting the much smaller Upper Marr Branch Falls, then carefully cross the stream. Then simply look for a user-created path through the woods and down to Marr Branch Falls. There are a few more waterfalls on Marr Branch, but accessing them legally is difficult.

Upper Fern Creek Falls

LOCATION: New River Gorge National River

ADDRESS/GPS FOR THE FALLS: County Road 82/Fayette Station Road; Upper Falls: 38° 3.498′ N, 81° 3.723′ W; directions to the other falls follow

DIRECTIONS: From the National Park Service's Canyon Rim Visitor Center in Lansing, turn right out of the parking lot and drive 0.2 mile. At the stop sign, make an extremely sharp right onto Lansing Loop Road and follow for 0.1 mile to a stop sign. Turn left onto County Road 82 (Fayette Station Rd) and follow for 0.3 mile to a pulloff on the right.

WEBSITE: None

WATERWAY: Fern Creek

HEIGHT: Varies **CREST:** Varies

NEAREST TOWN: Lansing

HIKE DIFFICULTY: Moderate

TRAIL QUALITY: Mostly dirt single-track

ROUND-TRIP DISTANCE: 1.8 miles to Upper Falls and back; 2.5 miles to Lower Falls and back

ADMISSION: None

TRIP REPORT & TIPS:

For the majority of the year, the Upper Falls of Fern Creek are mostly hidden from view, as the water is running through a cave-like cleft in the cliff wall. But, when the stream is rain swollen, the Upper Falls take on a dramatically different personality. Ed Rehbein, my good friend and coauthor of our book on New River Gorge waterfalls, adequately describes it as "High Drama." You'll hear the thunderous rumble of water well before you see it, and when you round the final bend in the trail, you'll stop in your tracks at the rugged beauty in front of you. Fern Creek leaps in spectacular fashion over the cleft into an amphitheater strewn with massive boulders—high drama indeed! While it only happens a few times a year, the drama is not to be missed if you can time it right. And if you happen to miss it, not to worry. There are a few more significant waterfalls downstream, with two of them featured on page 162. On the other hand, if you are fortunate to witness the Upper Falls as pictured, it's probably best not to attempt the downstream falls. They are in tight locations with little room to maneuver, so the spray from the high water flow would be hard to deal with.

Middle Fern Creek Falls

Lower Fern Creek Falls

TRIP REPORT (CONTINUED): From the pulloff along Route 82, you'll notice an obvious path leading steeply down into the woods. However, an easier route is found at the upper end of the pulloff. This old roadbed casually leads you to the base of the cliffs along a small stream. At a small seasonal waterfall, look around to see if you can spot the "Face in the Rock," a moss-covered stone carving of a man's face found on a small boulder. Once past the seasonal falls, the trail forks, with one route going sharply downhill, and the other bearing left. Take the left fork, and you'll soon be hugging the walls of the cliff on an easy-to-follow path forged by many years of climbers accessing the numerous climbing routes along the way. Follow for about 0.8 mile to Upper Fern Creek.

There are at least five significant waterfalls below the Upper Falls, with what I'll call the Middle and Lower Falls featured here. If you decide to make the rugged trek down to these, be aware that you'll be descending and then ascending on a dangerous and steep grade that requires a bit of bushwhacking. You'll also be dealing with several house-size boulders along the way—you'll need to work your way over or around these specimens to continue down the canyon. If you're still raring to go despite these warnings, the best route is to stay on the right side of the stream (looking downstream) as you descend. There are no official trails down into the canyon, but there's been enough traffic over the years that you should be able to pick up a faint path near the Middle Falls. Getting from the Upper Falls to the Middle Falls does require some bushwhacking, but you shouldn't have much trouble as long as you stay near the stream.

From the base of the Upper Falls, you'll reach the base of the Middle Falls at a little over 0.2 mile. Be careful here; there's very little wiggle room. The scramble down to the Lower Falls is a little easier to navigate. Some of the New River whitewater rafting guides will stop and allow the rafters to view the Lower and Middle Falls, so an unofficial path has been forged over the years. Of the three waterfalls pictured, the Lower Falls is my favorite. Hike down to the base of the falls for the best views. If you make the journey here in warmer months, keep a close eye out for copperheads, as I've seen quite a few of them on my treks down Fern Creek.

From the Middle Falls, the base of the Lower Falls is about 0.2 mile down the trail. One last warning shot—stay off of the railroad tracks you'll see beyond the Lower Falls. This is an extremely active rail line, and with the roar of Fern Creek and the New River, the trains will be on you before you know it.

Upper Falls of Craig Branch

LOCATION: New River Gorge National River

ADDRESS/GPS FOR THE FALLS: Arrowhead Trails Parking Area; 38° 2.524' N, 81° 3.468' W

DIRECTIONS: From US-19, follow WV-16 South through Fayetteville and take a left onto Gatewood Road. Follow for 2 miles and take a left onto Kaymoor Road. Follow for 0.9 mile, then turn right onto Arrowhead Road and follow for 0.2 mile to the parking area.

WEBSITE: None

WATERWAY: Craig Branch

HEIGHT: 85 feet **CREST:** Varies

NEAREST TOWN: Fayetteville

HIKE DIFFICULTY: Very strenuous

TRAIL QUALITY: The hike begins innocently enough on established trails, but it eventually turns into an off-trail bushwhack through dense rhododendron thickets and around small boulders

ROUND-TRIP DISTANCE: 1.9 miles from the Arrowhead Trail parking area to the lower falls and back

ADMISSION: None

TRIP REPORT & TIPS:

First and foremost, this waterfall adventure is a true bushwhack and should only be considered by experienced off-trail hikers. Once you leave the established park service trails, you're met with rhododendron thickets, massive boulders, and rock fields with deep holes hidden by thick leaf litter.

Craig Branch needs a lot of rain to make the difficult trek worthwhile. There are three ways to access the Upper Falls on Craig Branch, and none of them are easy. My preferred route is from the Arrowhead Trails Parking Area. The other two routes will be briefly detailed at the end of this listing.

From the Arrowhead Trail parking area, walk to the gravel road you drove in on, and pass around the gate. Stay on the road, which is now considered Craig Branch Trail, and follow for around 0.4 mile, and then turn left and enter into

Middle Craig Branch Falls

Lower Craig Branch Falls

TRIP REPORT (CONTINUED): the forest. Make your way off-trail 700 feet or so to these coordinates near the edge of the cliff: 38° 2.579′ N, 81° 3.598′ W. Here, you'll need to carefully look for a fallen tree leaning against the cliff wall and resting on dirt and rocks. Use this tree to assist you on your scramble down to the base of the cliffs. Once at the base, with your back facing the cliff you just scrambled down, turn right and follow along the base of the cliffs a short distance. You'll reach a couple massive boulders that you'll need to work your way around by going down the hill a bit, then climb back up to the base of the cliffs. Continue a short distance to the Upper Falls. If you want to ensure that there's enough water on Craig Branch to make the trek worthwhile, simply follow the road/Craig Branch Trail for 0.7 mile to a small bridge over the creek.

From the Upper Falls, work your way down into the canyon for about 0.1 mile to the Middle Falls. The going will surely be rough, and once you're at the Middle Falls, you'll have to crawl and fight through the rhododendron thickets to access the falls. Again, this is a true bushwhack and not for the faint of heart.

From the Middle Falls, bushwhack down into the canyon for around 90 yards to access the Lower Falls. Your route down from the Middle Falls will lead you away from the stream a bit, but work your way back toward the water on what appears to be an old service road choked with ferns and various weeds.

From here, simply backtrack the way you came. But, if you can't stomach the thought of backtracking, your exit strategy will be obvious to you once you see it. The Kaymoor Trail is just a few yards below the Lower Falls. Scramble down to the trail, and turn left. Follow the trail for about 0.5 mile, and at the old Kaymoor Mine site, pick up the Kaymoor Miner's Trail leading steeply up the mountain. Follow the Kaymoor Miner's Trail for a little over 0.3 mile to Kaymoor Top. Turn left and walk about 0.25 mile along the road to the Arrowhead Trails Parking Area. You can do this route in reverse and visit the Lower Falls first and bushwhack up to the Upper Falls. But, I prefer to start at the top and work my way down. If you decide to start with the Lower Falls, when you get to the "T" junction at the end of Kaymoor Road, turn left and drive a short distance to the Kaymoor Top parking area. You can't miss the trailhead for the Kaymoor Miner's Trail.

Upper Falls of Arbuckle Creek

LOCATION: New River Gorge National River

ADDRESS/GPS FOR THE FALLS: Arbuckle Trail; 37° 58.1'N, 81° 5.883'W

DIRECTIONS: From US-19 in Oak Hill, take the East Main Street exit. Turn onto Minden Road, and follow signs for ACE Adventure Resort about 3 miles away. Parking is available near a large information sign/map shortly after entering the ACE campus. The Arbuckle Trailhead is just a few yards back down the road.

WEBSITE: None

WATERWAY: Arbuckle Creek

HEIGHT: 15 feet **CREST:** Varies

NEAREST TOWN: Minden

HIKE DIFFICULTY: Easy, although the hike back to the trailhead will be uphill all the way

TRAIL QUALITY: Fair, with some soggy sections, exposed roots, and rocks

ROUND-TRIP DISTANCE: 1.2 miles

ADMISSION: None

TRIP REPORT & TIPS:

There are at least eight waterfalls on Arbuckle Creek, but I have yet to explore the stream above the Upper Falls. My friend Art was with me on my most recent hike here, and we're looking forward to going back for further upstream exploration.

From the trailhead at ACE Adventure Resort in Minden, hike gradually downhill for around 0.4 mile to a spur trail on the right. Follow the spur trail about 0.2 mile to the Upper Falls, where you'll find a nice vantage point from the trail. Carefully make your way down to the creek for images with the cascading stream in the foreground.

Double Falls

LOCATION: New River Gorge National River

ADDRESS/GPS FOR THE FALLS: Arbuckle Trail; 37° 57.888'N, 81° 5.515'W

DIRECTIONS: From US-19 in Oak Hill, take the East Main Street exit. Turn onto Minden Road, and follow signs for ACE Adventure Resort about 3 miles away. Parking available shortly after entering the ACE campus. The Arbuckle Trailhead is just a few yards back down the road.

WEBSITE: None

WATERWAY: Arbuckle Creek

HEIGHT: 40 feet, with a view of a 15-foot waterfall in the background **CREST:** Varies

NEAREST TOWN: Minden

HIKE DIFFICULTY: Easy, although the hike back to the trailhead is slightly uphill all the way

TRAIL QUALITY: Fair with some soggy sections, exposed roots, and rocks

ROUND-TRIP DISTANCE: 2.6 miles

ADMISSION: None

TRIP REPORT & TIPS:

This one is a treat! You'll have to do some scrambling to get down to the stream, but it's worth it. The pool area is quite large, so I prefer downstream vantage points that offer a better foreground. On your return, if you don't mind getting wet, hop into the stream above the double falls and creek-walk back to the Upper Falls; here you'll encounter at least five more waterfalls that can only be accessed via the creek.

From the trailhead, follow the Arbuckle Trail for 1.3 miles to access Double Falls.

The Little Brother

LOCATION: New River Gorge National River

ADDRESS/GPS FOR THE FALLS: County Road 25/Thurmond Road; 37° 56.183′ N, 81° 6.03′ W

DIRECTIONS: From US-19 South in Glen Jean, turn left at the stoplight (watch for New River Gorge National River signs), then left again onto WV-16/WV-61 North. Follow for 0.5 mile, then turn right, cross the bridge, and at the bank, turn left and follow toward the historic railroad town of Thurmond. Dunloup Creek will soon parallel County Road 25/Thurmond Road, and at 4.6 miles, look for a pullout on the right.

WEBSITE: None

WATERWAY: Dunloup Creek

HEIGHT: 7 feet **CREST:** Varies

NEAREST TOWN: Glen Jean

HIKE DIFFICULTY: Easy

TRAIL QUALITY: Narrow dirt path

ROUND-TRIP DISTANCE: 50 yards

ADMISSION: None

TRIP REPORT & TIPS:

Dunloup Creek Falls (page 152) receives most of the attention, and rightfully so, but its little brother is always fun to photograph and makes for a great add-on to your trip to Dunloup Creek Falls. From the large roadside pulloff, simply follow the unmarked path upstream about 20 yards to the falls. The creek bed is quite slippery, so be careful here. I typically only photograph this waterfall during or just after rain; the exposed portion of the shelf is rather unattractive when dry. I normally opt for compositions on the road side of the stream, but on occasion I have crossed the stream for alternate vantage points.

Glade Creek Falls

LOCATION: Babcock State Park

ADDRESS/GPS FOR THE FALLS: 486 Babcock Road, Clifftop, WV 25831; 37° 58.797′ N, 80° 56.788′ W

DIRECTIONS: Babcock State Park is easily accessible from Beckley and points south by following US-19 North. At the US-60 exit, travel east 10 miles to WV-41 South. The main entrance to the park is 2 miles south of Clifftop. Turn right into the park and stay straight, and in a short distance you will reach the parking area.

WEBSITE: babcocksp.com

WATERWAY: Glade Creek

HEIGHT: 15 feet **CREST:** Varies

NEAREST TOWN: Clifftop

HIKE DIFFICULTY: Roadside view

TRAIL QUALITY: Paved road

ROUND-TRIP DISTANCE: Roadside view, or short walks for various compositions

ADMISSION: None

TRIP REPORT & TIPS:

The iconic Glade Creek Grist Mill makes for a dramatic backdrop to the small stream-wide waterfall that's several yards downstream of the mill. The best vantage points for the waterfall and mill are from the road on the mill side of the stream, and you'll want to use your longer lens here. The other vantage point I suggest is from the parking area side of Glade Creek. Walk toward the park headquarters building, and follow the steps and walkway down to the stream. With the mill as the backdrop, this is a wonderful all-season waterfall.

Keeneys Creek Falls

LOCATION: New River Gorge National River

ADDRESS/GPS FOR THE FALLS: Keeneys Creek Road; 38° 1.965′ N, 81° 1.282′ W

DIRECTIONS: From Winona, follow Keeneys Creek Road for 2.3 miles, and look for a pullout on the left with space for 2–3 cars.

WEBSITE: None

WATERWAY: Keeneys Creek

HEIGHT: 12 feet **CREST:** Varies

NEAREST TOWN: Winona

HIKE DIFFICULTY: Roadside view, or easy, short scramble

TRAIL QUALITY: Roadside view or a rocky scramble down to the falls

ROUND-TRIP DISTANCE: Roadside view, or a few yards

ADMISSION: None

TRIP REPORT & TIPS:

Although recent severe flooding scoured Keeneys Creek and ruined several waterfalls, this one is still worthy of your visit, and I suggest that you return often to see if the other waterfalls come back to life.

From the pullout, walk down the road a few yards, hop the guardrail, and scramble a short distance down to the waterfall.

Note: On the drive to Keeneys Creek Falls, at about the 1.9-mile mark, look for a nice waterfall that is fun to shoot. You can get some nice shots from the bridge or hop the guardrail and scramble down.

Westerly Falls

LOCATION: Located between the Mossy and Mahan exits of I-64/I-77

ADDRESS/GPS FOR THE FALLS: County Road 15/ Milburn Road; 37° 59.59′ N, 81° 19.522′ W

DIRECTIONS: From Mossy, follow County Road 15/Milburn Road for 3.5 miles to the pulloff on the right.

WEBSITE: paintcreekwv.org/

WATERWAY: Paint Creek

HEIGHT: 5 feet **CREST:** Varies

NEAREST TOWN: Mossy

HIKE DIFFICULTY: Roadside view, or short scramble

TRAIL QUALITY: Roadside view, or short scramble via dirt path

ROUND-TRIP DISTANCE: Minimal

ADMISSION: None

TRIP REPORT & TIPS:

Paint Creek is a beautiful stream with many small cascades and old railroad trestles. I love visiting here during the spring when the blooming redbud and dogwood trees line the banks. Another great thing about a spring trip here is that you'll find water flowing across the entire ledge, which is much wider than shown here. A nice roadside view is available, but a short and relatively steep scramble down to the creek will offer much better perspectives.

Marsh Fork Falls

LOCATION: Twin Falls Resort State Park

ADDRESS/GPS FOR THE FALLS: Falls Trail Parking Area; 37° 37.182' N, 81° 27.35' W

DIRECTIONS: Twin Falls Resort State Park is located about 30 minutes from Beckley. From I-77 in Beckley, take the Robert C Byrd Drive/Mabscott exit (exit 42), and merge onto WV-16 South/WV-97 West/Robert C Byrd Drive and follow the signs to the park. After entering the park, turn right onto Cabin Creek Road, and then in 0.1 mile turn left and follow a short distance to the parking area.

WEBSITE: twinfallsresort.com

WATERWAY: Marsh Fork of Cabin Creek

HEIGHT: 15 feet **CREST:** Varies

NEAREST TOWN: Saulsville

HIKE DIFFICULTY: Easy

TRAIL QUALITY: Paved

ROUND-TRIP DISTANCE: 0.2 mile, unless combined with the hike to Black Fork Falls (below)

ADMISSION: None

TRIP REPORT & TIPS:

The watershed is very small, so you should time your visit in early to mid-spring or after a couple days of decent rain. Fallen trees somewhat mar the view as of the date of this book's publication, but hopefully it'll return to a more pristine condition soon.

Marsh Fork Falls is an easy walk on a paved path. From the parking area, follow the path for about 0.1 mile, then follow a paved spur trail a few feet and you'll reach an overlook at the top of the falls. A few more spur trails (unpaved) lead down to the creek.

Black Fork Falls

LOCATION: Twin Falls Resort State Park

ADDRESS/GPS FOR THE FALLS: Falls Trail Parking Area; 37° 37.098' N, 81° 26.98' W

DIRECTIONS: Twin Falls Resort State Park is about 30 minutes from Beckley. From I-77 in Beckley, take the Robert C Byrd Drive/Mabscott exit (exit 42), and merge onto WV-16 South/WV-97 West/Robert C Byrd Drive and follow the signs to the park. After entering the park, turn right onto Cabin Creek Road, and then in 0.1 mile turn left and follow a short distance to the parking area.

WEBSITE: twinfallsresort.com

WATERWAY: Black Fork of Cabin Creek

HEIGHT: 20 feet **CREST:** Varies

NEAREST TOWN: Saulsville

HIKE DIFFICULTY: Easy

TRAIL QUALITY: Rocky and soggy surface, with areas of exposed roots

ROUND-TRIP DISTANCE: 1.2 miles

ADMISSION: None

TRIP REPORT & TIPS:

Black Fork Falls is my favorite of the two waterfalls located within Twin Falls Resort State Park. Black Fork hurls over the ledge in a chute, with both sides of the creek offering picturesque views of the waterfall. I also like wading downstream a bit and composing a scene with water flowing through the frame.

From Marsh Fork Falls (page 174), follow the path to a fork, and bear right and follow the rocky path for about 0.5 mile. The trail will be above the stream, so you'll have to scramble a short distance down a spur trail for better photos

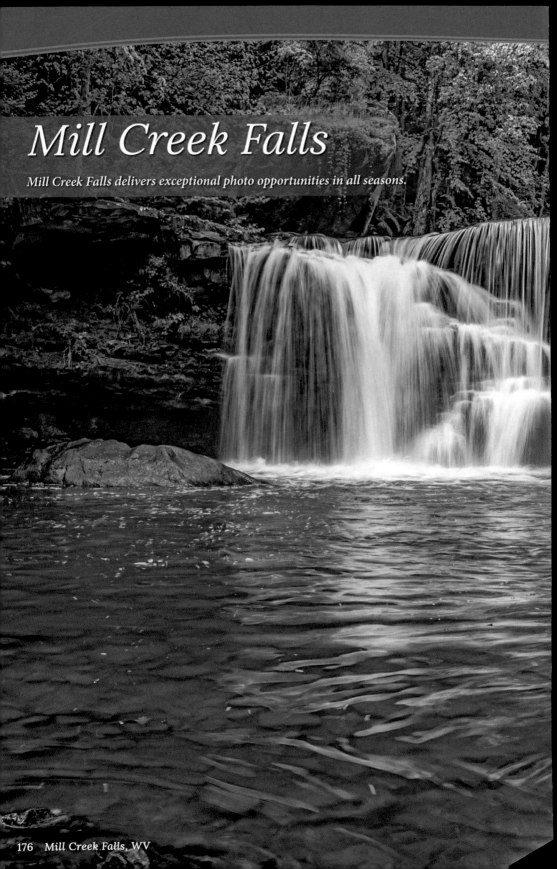

Mill Creek Falls

Mill Creek Falls delivers exceptional photo opportunities in all seasons.

Mill Creek Falls, WV

Mill Creek Falls

Mill Creek Falls is the highlight of this rugged mountain stream, but be sure to save time to explore many additional opportunities, both upstream and downstream from the falls.

LOCATION: Ansted Rail Trail

ADDRESS/GPS FOR THE FALLS: Hawks Nest Road; 38° 7.505′ N, 81° 6.464′ W

DIRECTIONS: From US-60 in Ansted, turn onto Page Street, which turns to the right and becomes Rich Creek Road, and follow for 0.3 mile. Then turn right onto Hawks Nest Road, and pass under US-60. The paved road will turn to gravel at a fork. Bear left here, and turn right at the next fork and cross the small bridge. Follow for 0.7 mile to a pullout on the left. The waterfall is 0.1 mile down the road.

WEBSITE: None

WATERWAY: Mill Creek

HEIGHT: 20 feet **CREST:** Varies

NEAREST TOWN: Ansted

HIKE DIFFICULTY: Roadside/trailside view, or a short, moderate scramble down to the creek

TRAIL QUALITY: A short dirt path with some tricky maneuvers over fallen trees near the bottom

ROUND-TRIP DISTANCE: Roadside view, or a few yards down to the stream

ADMISSION: None

TRIP REPORT & TIPS:

I've learned about a lot of waterfalls over the years from many different sources. One of the best sources before the advent of the internet, and even to this day, has been from kayakers. These guys and gals know where all the great falling water is, and many years ago while perusing a book about West Virginia whitewater, I saw a picture of Mill Creek Falls and went looking for it soon thereafter. Dozens of trips later, it still remains a favorite, and a spring or fall photography season isn't complete until I visit here. Fortunately, this waterfall is one of the highlights on my New River Gorge Photography Workshops, so I get to see it often and share its beauty with my workshop participants.

Raging floodwaters during the summer of 2016 made some changes to the pool below the falls, resulting in a few of my favorite spots no longer being an option. The pool is much larger now, but plenty of photo options remain. I especially enjoy shooting from downstream about 20 yards or so, using the rocky stream as my foreground. You'll want to save plenty of time to explore the many beautiful stream scenes and small cascades, both upstream and downstream of Mill Creek Falls.

While you can hike to this waterfall on the historic Ansted Rail Trail, it is much easier to access Mill Creek Falls from the road side of the stream. You'll want to park about 0.1 mile upstream of the waterfall so that your vehicle won't be in the field of view, and because that's the safest place for you to park on this narrow road. From your vehicle, walk down the road a short distance, and after you pass the waterfall, you'll see an obvious path down to the stream. This path is short, but it's a steep, narrow, and often slick scramble, so proceed with caution.

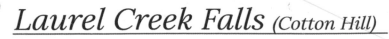

Laurel Creek Falls (Cotton Hill)

LOCATION: WV-16 between Fayetteville and Gauley Bridge

ADDRESS/GPS FOR THE FALLS: WV-16/Beckwith Road; 38° 6.635' N, 81° 8.807' W

DIRECTIONS: From Fayetteville, follow WV-16 North for a little over 6 miles, and look for a pullout with room for 3 cars on the left side of the road.

WEBSITE: None

WATERWAY: Laurel Creek

HEIGHT: 25 feet **CREST:** Varies

NEAREST TOWN: Beckwith

HIKE DIFFICULTY: Roadside view, or a moderate scramble to the falls

TRAIL QUALITY: Roadside view, or a steep rocky scramble

ROUND-TRIP DISTANCE: 40 yards

ADMISSION: None

TRIP REPORT & TIPS:

The stretch of Laurel Creek that parallels WV-16 actually offers more than just the one waterfall featured. Unfortunately, parking is limited, and there are no trails that keep you away from the busy roadway. I'm featuring this one because not only is it the tallest on the stream, but also because it's one you can access somewhat safely.

I've listed it as having a roadside view, but to get a really good shot of this waterfall, you'll need to make a steep scramble down a bank with many large and loose rocks, and you'll need to navigate through weeds and trees.

From the roadside pullout, walk down the road a few yards while avoiding traffic. For the most part, you can walk on the stream side of the guardrail for a little bit of safety. Route 16 is a busy road, and folks are typically driving relatively fast through here, so be careful and alert while near the road. I usually begin my descent to the creek about 10–15 feet downstream of the falls. If you decide to get in the creek, be warned that the rocks and streambed are very slick.

You can walk upstream from your vehicle for the other waterfalls; one is easily visible from the road at 0.3 mile from the pullout, while the other one is hidden from view, and is 0.4 mile from the pullout.

Cathedral Falls

LOCATION: Gauley Bridge

ADDRESS/GPS FOR THE FALLS: US-60, Gauley Bridge; 38° 9.255′N, 81° 10.756′W

DIRECTIONS: From the bridge over the Gauley River in Gauley Bridge, follow US-60 east for 1 mile, and the parking area will be on the left.

WEBSITE: None

WATERWAY: Cane Branch

HEIGHT: Drops around 60 feet over steep cascades **CREST:** Varies

NEAREST TOWN: Gauley Bridge

HIKE DIFFICULTY: Roadside view

TRAIL QUALITY: Roadside view

ROUND-TRIP DISTANCE: Roadside view

ADMISSION: None

TRIP REPORT & TIPS:

The waters of Cane Branch cascade steeply down a series of ledges into a natural amphitheater surrounded by a narrow canyon, with the towering walls on either side giving one a feeling of being in a cathedral. Cathedral Falls is one of the tallest and most visited waterfalls in West Virginia.

Located right off of US-60, you can step out of your vehicle and start taking photographs; Cathedral Falls is that close. The roadside location and sheer beauty of the falls virtually ensures that you'll be sharing the falls with others. I've found that visiting early in the morning or on rainy days increases my chances of finding rare solitude at this beautiful waterfall. Photographing here during or just after rain is best; for some reason, the rocks here just look really weird and unattractive when dry.

While you're in the area, follow US-60 west for about 3 miles through the town of Glen Ferris to a couple more waterfalls. One is the river-wide Kanawha Falls, which has several distinct segments of 15 feet or so. Parking is available at a small park near the falls. Lastly, about 0.1 mile from Kanawha Falls is a small waterfall on Riggs Branch, tucked away in a little canyon across the road from a Department of Highways facility.

Ramsey Branch Falls

LOCATION: Off of Ramsey Branch Road in Gauley River rafting country

ADDRESS/GPS FOR THE FALLS: Ramsey Branch Road; 38° 12.061'N, 81° 0.747'W

DIRECTIONS: From Fayetteville, cross the New River Gorge Bridge, and then follow for about 5 miles and take the US-60 exit. At the stop sign, turn right and follow US-60 4.6 miles west to Saturday Road on the right. Follow Saturday Road for almost 8 miles, and turn left onto Ramsey Branch Road, and follow for 1.6 miles to just above the Gauley River. Take a right turn here, and after a very short distance there is a road to the right, which drops down to Ramsey Branch. Follow this road a few yards to a hairpin turn at creek level and park here. Please be aware that the last 0.5 mile or so of Ramsey Branch Road is quite steep and not suitable for the family sedan; you'll need a vehicle with good clearance to navigate the ruts, potholes, etc.

WEBSITE: None

WATERWAY: Ramsey Branch

HEIGHT: 30 feet **CREST:** Varies

NEAREST TOWN: Hico

HIKE DIFFICULTY: Moderate

TRAIL QUALITY: Rough, due to fallen trees and stream crossings

ROUND-TRIP DISTANCE: 0.25 mile

ADMISSION: None

TRIP REPORT & TIPS:

Ramsey Branch Falls is a hidden gem nestled among a beautiful hardwood forest surrounded by lush ferns and rhododendron. The trek to the falls is short, but due to a couple stream crossings, fallen trees, and the above-mentioned rhododendron, you need to take your time and be aware of the difficulties. The route to the waterfall is getting easier to follow as more people visit, but if you lose the path or find yourself questioning if there is actually a path, just follow the stream: you can't miss the spectacular Ramsey Branch Falls. You'll find that great compositions can be had from either side of the stream, as well as in the nice cascading stream featured here.

From the parking area, follow the short, unofficial trail upstream to the falls. Farther upstream, but not listed here, is a nice 10–12 foot waterfall, with access best gained by a roadside scramble.

Laurel Creek Falls

LOCATION: Gauley River rafting territory

ADDRESS/GPS FOR THE FALLS: Access Road; 38° 12.857' N, 81° 1.77' W

DIRECTIONS: From Fayetteville, cross the New River Gorge Bridge, and then follow for about 5 miles and take the US-60 exit. At the stop sign, turn right and follow US-60 4.6 miles west to Saturday Road on the right. Follow Saturday Road for 6.4 miles, and take a sharp left onto Lucas Road and continue for 1 mile. At a sharp left turn, bear right and leave the hardtop for a gravel access road that follows Laurel Creek and leads down to the Gauley River. There are a few junctions along this route, so always choose the route that heads downhill following Laurel Creek. After a couple miles, you'll reach a towering sandstone cliff and an old wooden structure. Park here.

WEBSITE: None

WATERWAY: Laurel Creek

HEIGHT: 30 feet **CREST:** Varies

NEAREST TOWN: Hico

HIKE DIFFICULTY: Strenuous scramble

TRAIL QUALITY: Steep scramble on loose rocks and soil

ROUND-TRIP DISTANCE: 0.25 mile

ADMISSION: None.

TRIP REPORT & TIPS:

This one is a waterfall photographer's dream and one of my favorites. While you can capture a decent image from an overlook above the falls, if you're able, you should make the crazy scramble down to stream level. Be very cautious, though, as there are no official trails down, and the going is tough. I typically walk down the road 25 yards or so to a drainage ditch and carefully make my way to the stream via the ditch. There are so many photo opportunities here, and I like to work on some downstream compositions before making my way upstream to the falls.

While not listed in this book, you can see several smaller waterfalls by creek-walking upstream from the waterfall. And downstream from the waterfall there are quite a few beautiful cascades before Laurel Creek passes through a railroad culvert and empties into the Gauley River.

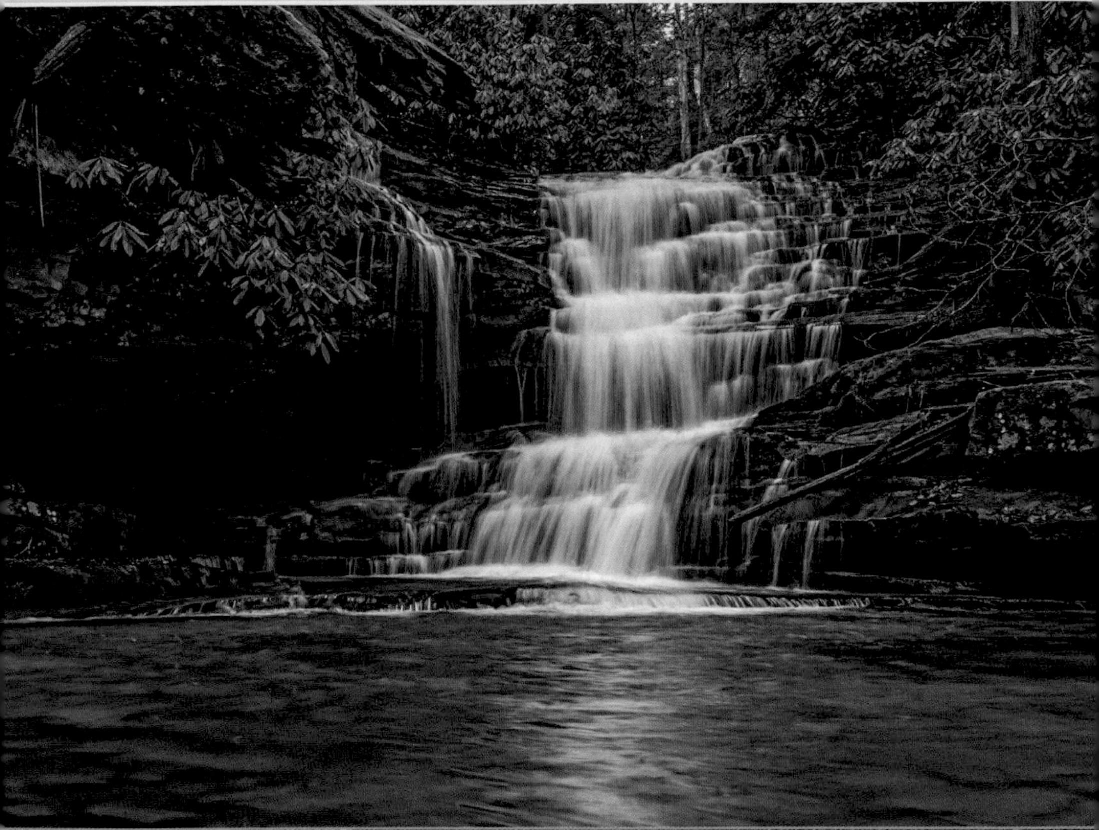

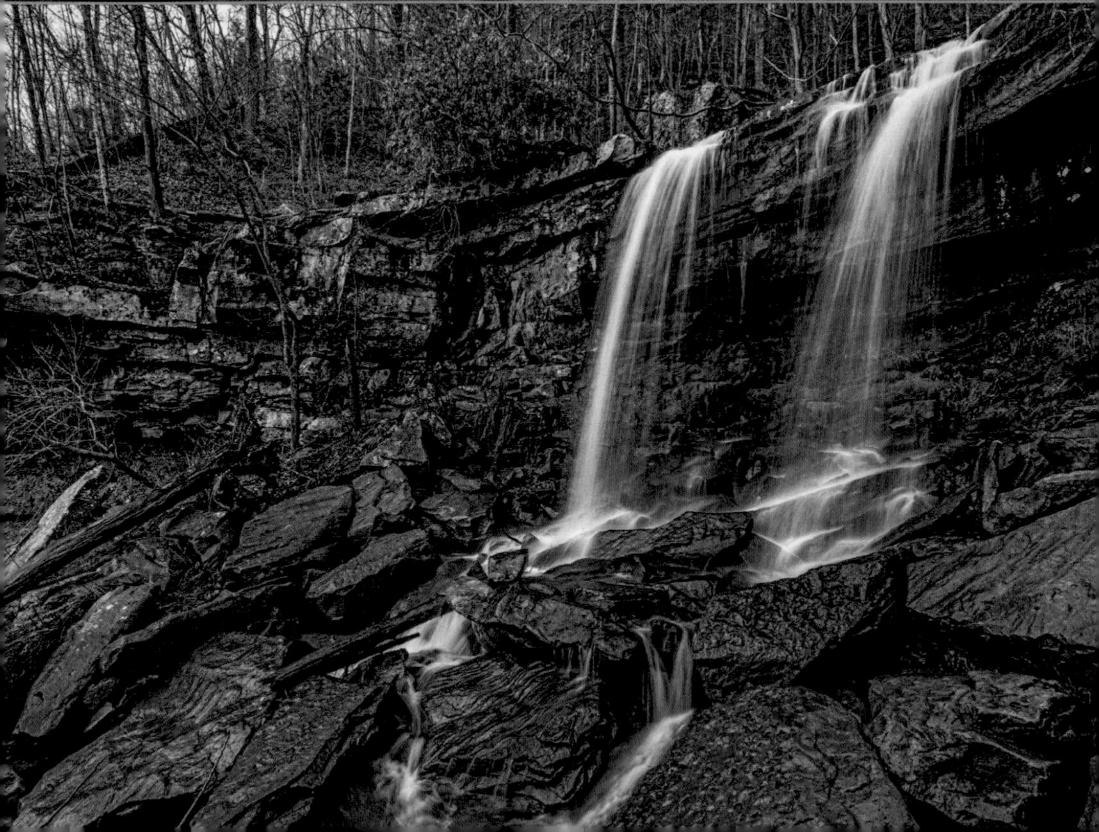

Upper Turkey Creek Falls

LOCATION: Hawks Nest State Park

ADDRESS/GPS FOR THE FALLS: Cliffside Trail;
38° 7.404'N, 81° 7.784'W

DIRECTIONS: From the Hawks Nest State Park
Lodge parking area, turn left onto US-60 West
and follow for 0.4 mile to the Hawks Nest Overlook parking area on the left.

WEBSITE: None

WATERWAY: Turkey Creek

HEIGHT: 20 feet **CREST:** Varies

NEAREST TOWN: Ansted

HIKE DIFFICULTY: Moderate

TRAIL QUALITY: Fair to poor in sections,
due to narrow track, soggy sections, and a few
downed trees

ROUND-TRIP DISTANCE: 0.8 mile

ADMISSION: None

TRIP REPORT & TIPS:

My buddy Art joined me on this hike on
an early-spring afternoon, and we found
it with great water flow. You can catch a
glimpse of the falls from the trail, but to
get decent shots, you'll need to scramble
down to the creek.

The trailhead is found near the end of
the parking area, and the trail quickly
descends into the woods. At 0.2 mile
you'll reach Turkey Creek, and after a
sharp left, the trail parallels the stream for
another 0.2 mile to the waterfall, with a
nice set of cascades along the way. Not
counting the Lower Falls (next listing),
there are two more waterfalls downstream a bit, but due to space constraints
and dangerous access, they are not
featured in this book.

Lower Turkey Creek Falls

LOCATION: Hawks Nest State Park

ADDRESS/GPS FOR THE FALLS: Fisherman's Trail;
38° 7.279'N, 81° 7.802'W

DIRECTIONS: From US-60 in Ansted, turn onto
Page Street, which turns to the right and becomes
Rich Creek Road, and follow for 0.3 mile. Then
turn right onto Hawks Nest Road, and pass under
US-60. The paved road will turn to gravel at a fork.
Bear left here, and turn right at the next fork and
cross the small bridge. Follow another 1.8 miles to
a parking area.

WEBSITE: None

WATERWAY: Turkey Creek

HEIGHT: 30 feet **CREST:** Varies

NEAREST TOWN: Ansted

HIKE DIFFICULTY: Easy

TRAIL QUALITY: Hard-packed dirt

ROUND-TRIP DISTANCE: 1 mile

ADMISSION: None

TRIP REPORT & TIPS:

A pleasant 0.5-mile stroll along the lake on
one side and the steep cliffs on the other
side lead to this beautiful waterfall in a
rugged and boulder-strewn setting.

From the parking lot, simply follow the
trail for 0.5 mile to the waterfall. You'll get
a nice view of the Hawks Nest Dam, and
there are several nice vantage points on
either side of the waterfall. Turkey Creek
needs a fair amount of rain to look good,
so be sure to plan your trips accordingly.
You can also ride the tram down from
Hawks Nest State Park and walk from the
tram to the parking lot, and on to the falls.

Panther Creek Falls

LOCATION: Gauley River National Recreation Area

ADDRESS/GPS FOR THE FALLS: Mason's Branch River Access; 38° 13.431′ N, 80° 59.388′ W

DIRECTIONS: At the junction of US-19 and WV-129 in Mount Nebo, turn onto WV-129 toward Summersville Dam. Go 9.9 miles west toward Drennen, and take a left onto Panther Mountain Road (County Road 22) in the town of Poe. Follow 3.7 miles to the Mason's Branch public access area sign, then turn left and go another 1.1 miles down to the parking/boat launch areas.

WEBSITE: None

WATERWAY: Panther Creek

HEIGHT: 25 feet **CREST:** Varies

NEAREST TOWN: Mount Nebo

HIKE DIFFICULTY: Easy

TRAIL QUALITY: Rocky single-track with a stream crossing

ROUND-TRIP DISTANCE: 100 yards

ADMISSION: None

TRIP REPORT & TIPS:

I stumbled on Panther Creek Falls while searching for nice views of the Gauley River. I returned later with my buddy Art and enjoyed great photography conditions.

From the parking area, walk down the road a short distance toward the Gauley River. Follow the road over a concrete bridge. After a very short distance, look to your left, and you can't miss the obvious path into the woods. Follow the path to the creek, and cross to the left of the pool and small cascade, then clamber up a ledge and continue up and around to the waterfall through a notch between the mountainside and a large rock column.

Bucklick Branch Falls

LOCATION: Gauley River National Recreation Area

ADDRESS/GPS FOR THE FALLS: River access road off of Panther Mountain Road; 38° 14.166′ N, 81° 1.632′ W

DIRECTIONS: At the junction of US-19 and WV-129 in Mount Nebo, turn onto WV-129 toward Summersville Dam. Go 9.9 miles west toward Drennen, and take a left onto Panther Mountain Road (County Road 22) in the town of Poe. Follow for 5.2 miles and watch for a spur road on the left. You'll need a vehicle with good clearance on the road down to Bucklick Branch. Follow the spur road for 0.2 mile, and you'll soon reach Bucklick Branch. If possible, drive through the creek to a large area that makes for a good parking spot.

WEBSITE: None

WATERWAY: Bucklick Branch

HEIGHT: 12 feet **CREST:** Varies

NEAREST TOWN: Mount Nebo

HIKE DIFFICULTY: Moderate; uphill return hike

TRAIL QUALITY: A rutted, muddy, steep section of road down to the river

ROUND-TRIP DISTANCE: A few hundred yards

ADMISSION: None

TRIP REPORT & TIPS:

Bucklick Branch has been on my radar for several years. When I finally visited, I found the waterfall to be quite beautiful, but the setting is even better, with outstanding views of the Gauley River rushing by yards away from the waterfall.

To reach the waterfall from where you parked, wade back across Bucklick Branch and follow the dirt road 100 yards or so to the Gauley River; you can't miss it.

Upper Falls of Holly River

LOCATION: Holly River State Park

ADDRESS/GPS FOR THE FALLS: Left Fork Holly River Road; 38° 38.137′ N, 80° 19.21′ W

DIRECTIONS: After exiting the main park entrance, turn left onto WV-20 and follow south for 1.3 miles, and then turn left onto the gravel Left Fork Holly River Road/County Road 3. Follow for 4.2 miles, and turn right at the sign for Upper Falls, Potato Knob, and Shupe's Chute. The parking area is a few yards down the road and to the right.

WEBSITE: hollyriver.com

WATERWAY: Fall Run

HEIGHT: 15 feet **CREST:** Varies

NEAREST TOWN: Hacker Valley

HIKE DIFFICULTY: Easy

TRAIL QUALITY: A short walk on a gravel road, and then a wooden boardwalk with steps

ROUND-TRIP DISTANCE: 0.4 mile

ADMISSION: None

TRIP REPORT & TIPS:

The Upper Falls is nestled in a little cove and surrounded by rhododendron, evergreens, and moss-covered rocks and boulders. Plenty of vantage points to photograph the Upper Falls are available, and I especially enjoy the longer views from the middle of the creek, with the water cascading over the rocks as my foreground.

From the parking area, walk back up the road a bit to the trail and boardwalk down to the falls. If the boardwalk is wet, be careful—I've almost fallen on the slippery steps several times.

Note: In addition to the Lower Falls (page 194), Holly River State Park is home to Shupe's Chute and at least three additional waterfalls. Pick up a park trail map for routes to these three waterfalls, but try to go after a lot of rain.

Lower Falls of Holly River

LOCATION: Holly River State Park

ADDRESS/GPS FOR THE FALLS: Left Fork Holly River Road; 38°38'6.16"N, 80°19'30.21"W

DIRECTIONS: After exiting the main park entrance, turn left onto WV-20 and follow south for 1.3 miles, and then turn left onto the gravel Left Fork Holly River Road/County Road 3. Follow for 4.2 miles, and turn right at the sign for Upper Falls, Potato Knob, and Shupe's Chute. The parking area is a few yards down the road and to the right.

WEBSITE: hollyriver.com

WATERWAY: Left Fork Holly River

HEIGHT: 10 feet **CREST:** Varies

NEAREST TOWN: Hacker Valley

HIKE DIFFICULTY: Moderate, due to stream crossing and scramble

TRAIL QUALITY: Wide gravel path to the stream crossing, then more of a soggy single-track

ROUND-TRIP DISTANCE: 0.9 mile

ADMISSION: None

TRIP REPORT & TIPS:

The surroundings here are gorgeous: lush and green even in late winter.

From the parking area, follow the signs to Shupe's Chute and Potato Knob. When you reach the sign for Shupe's Chute straight ahead, don't follow it; instead, bear to the right on the path you're on. After a few yards the trail ends at the river. Carefully cross the stream and pick up the trail and follow the river downstream a short distance to the Lower Falls. After that, walk back up the trail, but instead of crossing the river, continue upriver until you see Shupe's Chute, where Fall Run is squeezed into a narrow chute.

Wildcat Falls

LOCATION: Near the community of Ireland

ADDRESS/GPS FOR THE FALLS: Wildcat Road; 38° 47.2'N, 80° 26.683'W

DIRECTIONS: From Ireland, turn onto Wildcat Road and follow for about 2.5 miles, and turn right onto Green Hill Road. After a few yards look for a pulloff on the left, and park.

WEBSITE: None

WATERWAY: Glady Creek

HEIGHT: 15 feet **CREST:** Varies

NEAREST TOWN: Ireland

HIKE DIFFICULTY: Easy

TRAIL QUALITY: Dirt road

ROUND-TRIP DISTANCE: 0.1 mile

ADMISSION: None

TRIP REPORT & TIPS:

My buddy Curt scouted this one for me, and we both enjoyed our visits to this neat little waterfall. Glady Creek is rather narrow here and surrounded by both native and nonnative plants/bushes, so your composition options are somewhat limited. Since it is only 45 minutes away, you can combine Wildcat Falls with a Holly River State Park visit. It's also conveniently located near Falls Mill (page 196).

From the pulloff, enter a small woodsy area to the left, and follow an old dirt road about 0.05 mile down to the stream. Work your way through the brush and over some rocks to the large boulder shown in the above image.

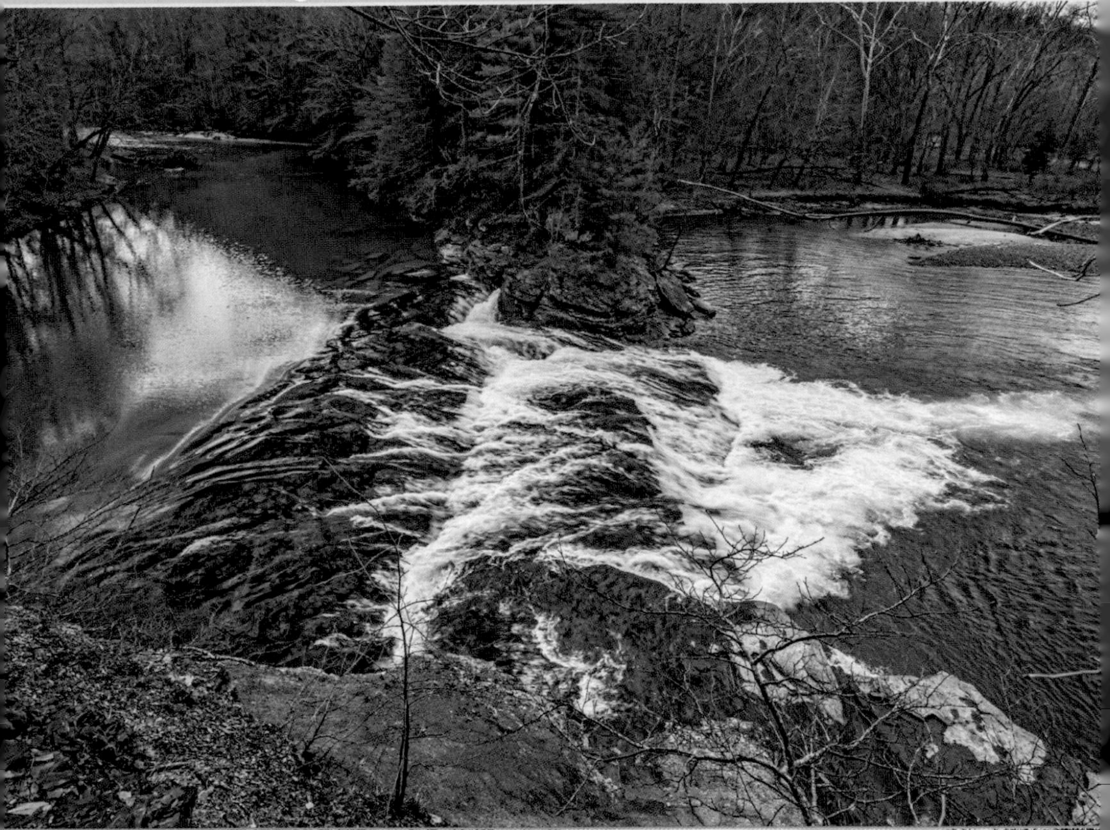

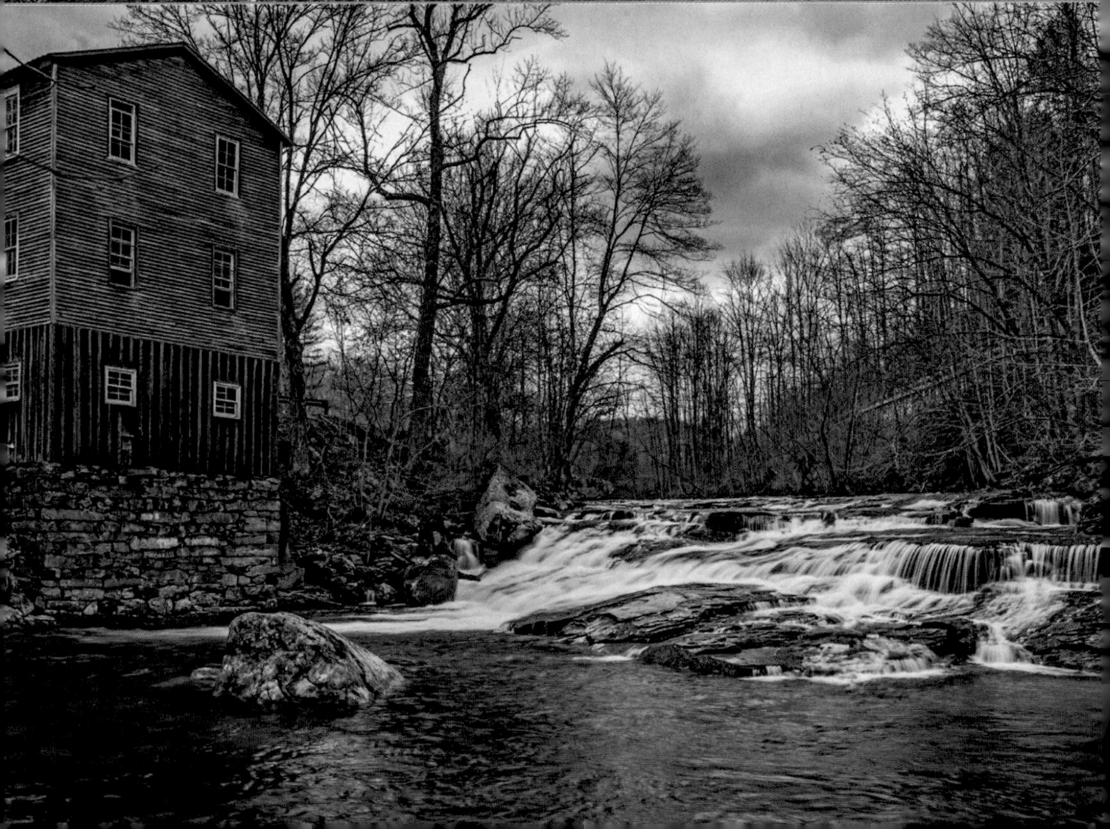

Falls Mill Falls

LOCATION: Upstream limit of Burnsville Lake

ADDRESS/GPS FOR THE FALLS: Pleasant Hill Road; 38° 46.449′ N, 80° 33.067′ W

DIRECTIONS: From Flatwoods, follow US-19 North for 10.5 miles, and then turn right onto Green Hill Road. In a few yards, turn right onto Pleasant Hill Road. A parking area with restrooms is on the left.

WEBSITE: None

WATERWAY: Little Kanawha River

HEIGHT: 5 feet **CREST:** 50 feet

NEAREST TOWN: Falls Mill

HIKE DIFFICULTY: Easy

TRAIL QUALITY: Good

ROUND-TRIP DISTANCE: 100 yards

ADMISSION: None

TRIP REPORT & TIPS:

While not an impressive waterfall height-wise, the waterfall at Falls Mill is quite pretty. I prefer the vantage point from above the falls, and if you visit here under the right conditions, you can capture some beautiful photographs beneath a nice cloudy sky. The compositions from stream level are nice as well, but no matter your vantage point, you have to be careful to eliminate fencing from a nearby baseball field.

From the parking area, it's a short walk to the upper viewing area; just follow the obvious path. Walk around the outcropping to access stream-level views of Falls Mill. Wildcat Falls, featured on page 194, is only a 15- to 20-minute drive from Falls Mill.

Arlington Falls at Fidlers Mill

LOCATION: Along WV-20 and Heaston Ridge Road in Arlington

ADDRESS/GPS FOR THE FALLS: Heaston Ridge Road; 38° 47.955′ N, 80°20′48.36″W

DIRECTIONS: From Buckhannon, follow WV-20 South for 17 miles to a right turn on Heaston Ridge Road/County Road 20/15, and follow a few feet to the mill. Parking at Fidler's Mill is on the left, just after passing the mill.

WEBSITE: None

WATERWAY: Little Kanawha River

HEIGHT: 10 feet **CREST:** Varies

NEAREST TOWN: Arlington

HIKE DIFFICULTY: Easy

TRAIL QUALITY: Fair

ROUND-TRIP DISTANCE: Roadside

ADMISSION: None

TRIP REPORT & TIPS:

The historic Fidler's Mill is the highlight of this waterfall stop. A smaller mill was originally constructed in 1821; it was enlarged in the 1840s after being purchased by William Fidler. The mill is a beautiful structure and certainly enhances Arlington Falls.

From the parking area, simply follow a muddy path down to a jumble of logs and branches collected by storm waters. Carefully work your way over the log jumble to a large boulder for the straight-on shot shown here. The muddy path leads on down to the stream if you wish to explore other options. Arlington Falls is a great add-on to a trip to Holly River State Park; it's only 30 minutes from the park.

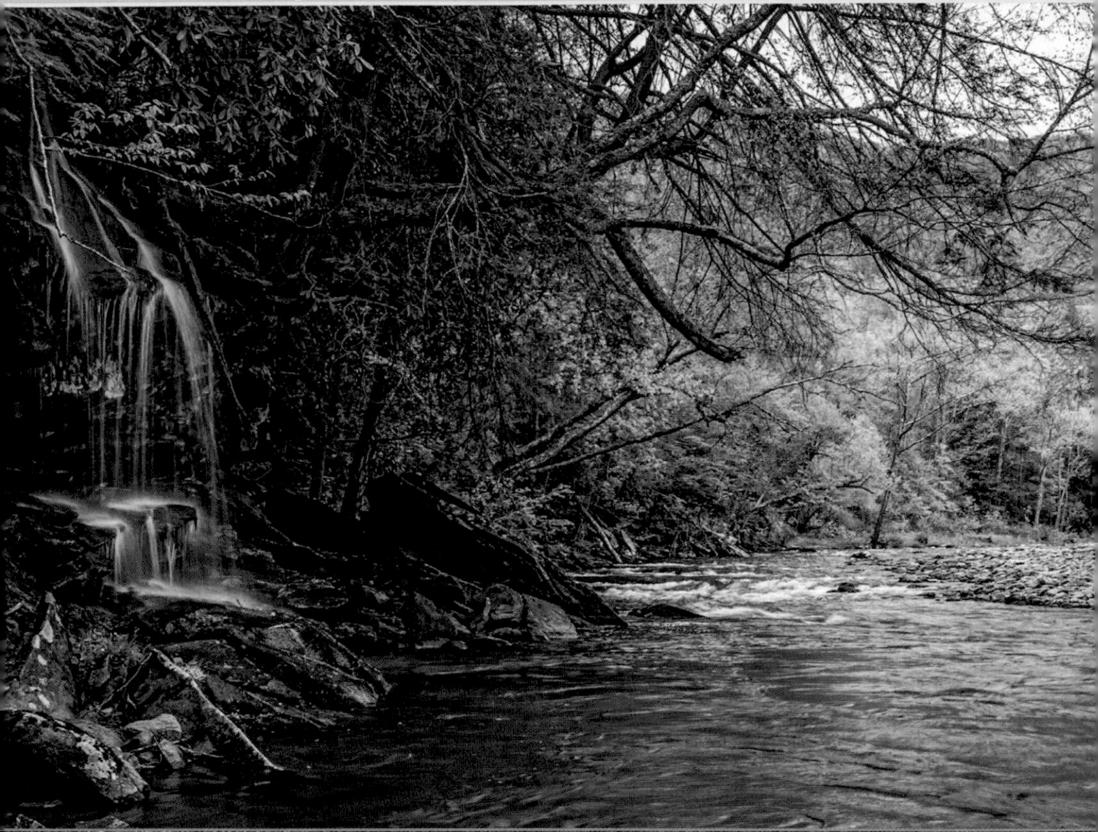

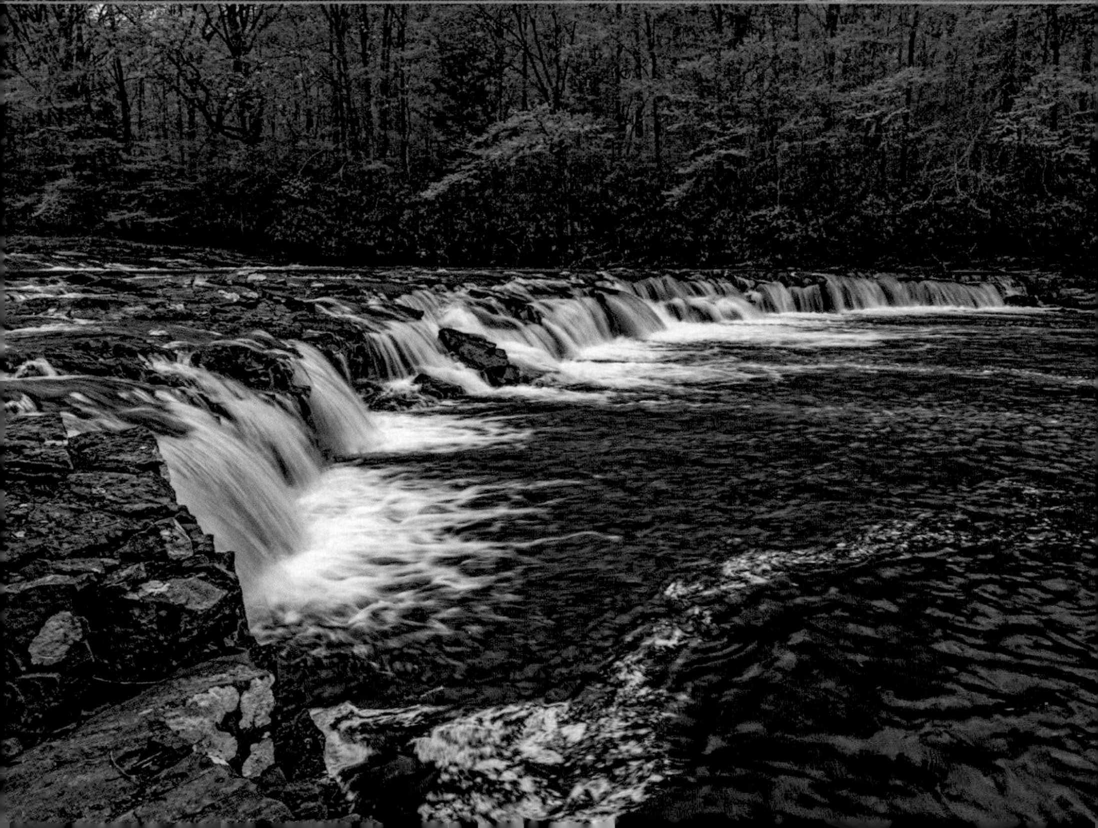

Little Run Falls

LOCATION: Webster County

ADDRESS/GPS FOR THE FALLS: Bergoo Road; 38° 31.367′ N, 80° 14.677′ W

DIRECTIONS: From Bergoo, follow Bergoo Road for a little over 5 miles, and look for a parking pullout on the right.

WEBSITE: None

WATERWAY: Little Run

HEIGHT: 12 feet **CREST:** Varies

NEAREST TOWN: Bergoo

HIKE DIFFICULTY: Short but steep roadside scramble

TRAIL QUALITY: Packed dirt

ROUND-TRIP DISTANCE: 15 yards

ADMISSION: None

TRIP REPORT & TIPS:

As I was finishing up my shoot at Whitaker Falls (below), a fisherman walked over and struck up a conversation with me. He obviously knew the area and was sharing some great locations with me. One in particular was this fun waterfall on Little Run, which he led me to and then went on his way. I was mesmerized by the view before me; a stream emptying into the river as a waterfall, and the majestic Elk River rounding out the scene. It doesn't get much better than this!

Park alongside the road at an obvious pullout, and carefully scramble down the short, steep bank, then work your way upstream for a closer view.

Whitaker Falls

LOCATION: Webster County

ADDRESS/GPS FOR THE FALLS: Bergoo Road; 38° 31.518′ N, 80° 11.038′ W

DIRECTIONS: From Bergoo, follow Bergoo Road for 9.2 miles. The waterfall and parking will be on the right side of the road.

WEBSITE: None

WATERWAY: Elk River

HEIGHT: 6 feet **CREST:** Varies

NEAREST TOWN: Bergoo

HIKE DIFFICULTY: Roadside

TRAIL QUALITY: Roadside

ROUND-TRIP DISTANCE: A few feet

ADMISSION: None

TRIP REPORT & TIPS:

Hard to beat a river-wide waterfall, especially when the river is as beautiful as this one. A haven for folks who enjoy fishing, the Elk River is also a gem for photographers, with many incredible scenes to choose from. While only a 6-foot drop, Whitaker Falls is a pretty waterfall in an incredible setting.

Park along the road on a pullout, and work your way down to the river and the falls.

Left Fork Falls

LOCATION: Webster County

ADDRESS/GPS FOR THE FALLS: Public Road 26/4; 38° 27.835' N, 80° 14.577' W

DIRECTIONS: From Bergoo, turn right onto Leatherwood Road, and follow for about 1 mile. Then take a slight left onto an unnamed road that Google indicates is Public Road 26/4. Follow this road for about 2 miles. Then the road makes a sharp left here and begins going steeply uphill. If you don't have a high clearance vehicle, I advise you to park here and walk this final mile.

WEBSITE: None

WATERWAY: Leatherwood Creek

HEIGHT: 15 feet **CREST:** Varies

NEAREST TOWN: Bergoo

HIKE DIFFICULTY: Roadside scramble if you drive, but a moderate uphill walk if you hike in

TRAIL QUALITY: Roadside scramble on loose soil; if you hike in, add a rocky, rutted road to the description

ROUND-TRIP DISTANCE: 20 yards if you drove or 2 miles if you hike

ADMISSION: None

TRIP REPORT & TIPS:

This rugged stream has at least two good-sized waterfalls, with one about 100 yards downstream of the one I've featured.

From the sharp left turn a mile down the road, determine if you want to make the drive up the hill to this beauty. My SUV had no trouble, but I'd leave the family sedan at the bottom and hike up.

Note: You probably should avoid this area during Labor Day weekend due to large crowds associated with an ATV event.

Lincamp Branch Falls

LOCATION: Monongahela National Forest

ADDRESS/GPS FOR THE FALLS: Forest Road; 38° 21.917' N, 80° 30.892' W

DIRECTIONS: From Cowan, follow WV-20 North through town, and after a little over 1 mile, make a slight right onto Williams River Road and follow for around 0.4 mile, then turn right to remain on Williams River Road. Follow for another 4 miles and turn right onto Forest Road 101. Cross the bridge and follow for 0.1 mile, then turn right and follow an unnamed road for 4.4 miles to the waterfall.

WEBSITE: None

WATERWAY: Lincamp Branch

HEIGHT: A small drop and then a larger drop, totaling around 12 feet **CREST:** Varies

NEAREST TOWN: Cowen

HIKE DIFFICULTY: Easy

TRAIL QUALITY: Packed dirt

ROUND-TRIP DISTANCE: 20 yards

ADMISSION: None

TRIP REPORT & TIPS:

I love spending time in the Monongahela National Forest, and Lincamp Branch Falls afforded me the perfect opportunity to explore part of the forest I hadn't visited before. While a Gauley River tributary, I placed it in this chapter due to its proximity to other waterfalls in the region.

Just after you pass the waterfall, you can park along the road, or look for a road to the left that leads up to an obvious camping spot. Park here and walk a few yards down to the falls.

Blackwater Falls

River-level views of the majestic Blackwater Falls are worth the steep scramble down into the canyon!

Blackwater Falls

Blackwater Falls is one of the highest and most spectacular West Virginia Waterfalls.

LOCATION: Blackwater Falls State Park

ADDRESS/GPS FOR THE FALLS: Gentle Trail Trailhead parking; river-level view: 39° 6.763′N, 79° 28.899′W

DIRECTIONS: From the park entrance, continue driving straight until reaching a stop sign, bear left, and cross the bridge spanning the Blackwater River. Parking for the Gentle Trail is just up the hill on the right, and across the road from a park service area.

WEBSITE: blackwaterfalls.com

WATERWAY: Blackwater River

HEIGHT: 60 feet **CREST:** Varies

NEAREST TOWN: Davis

HIKE DIFFICULTY: A strenuous descent/ascent on an unofficial trail

TRAIL QUALITY: Hard-packed dirt, with rocks and exposed roots

ROUND-TRIP DISTANCE: 0.5 mile

ADMISSION: None

TRIP REPORT & TIPS:

Most photographs of Blackwater Falls are captured from one of two outstanding vantage points on either side of the canyon. But there is one more place to view this incredible waterfall. From the upper end of the Gentle Trail parking area, you'll see a sign warning of the dangers of entering the canyon. The path down to the river begins here at the sign.

If you still want to venture down to the river after reading the warning sign near the parking area, it's very simple. Kayakers use this trail to put in for their Blackwater River runs, and over time, the path has become well-worn and easy to follow. I rate this as strenuous, due to several factors, but the walk down is quite easy until the last few feet; that's where you have to make a bit of a scramble down to the river. Take in the long views first, then things get strenuous. If the water is low enough, you can rock hop and boulder climb your way upstream for closer views, but be careful; a stumble on the extremely slick rocks will have you in the swift-moving current before you know it. If you do travel on upstream, you won't have to backtrack unless you just want to. About 20 yards or so from the falls, you should be able to pick out a path leading into the woods to the right; on my last visit, this path was marked by a blue ribbon. Simply follow the path back up the hillside and you'll eventually reach the Gentle Trail viewing platform. Be warned though that this trail is very steep and narrow.

While venturing down into the canyon is discouraged by park staff, it is not illegal. But it is dangerous, due to the river current.

Note: Your safety is your responsibility, so be extra cautious if you decide to make the trek. If you're at all unsure about it, just stay up top and enjoy the views from the two official viewing platforms (pages 206, 210).

Blackwater Falls:
Gentle Trail Overlook

From the overlook, you'll have a bird's-eye view of this wondrous waterfall.

Blackwater Falls: Gentle Trail Overlook

Four seasons of amazing views await you from this easy-to-access overlook.

LOCATION: Blackwater Falls State Park

ADDRESS/GPS FOR THE FALLS: Gentle Trail Trailhead Parking; 39° 6.798′ N, 79° 28.867′ W

DIRECTIONS: From the park entrance, continue driving straight until reaching a stop sign, bear left, and cross the bridge spanning the Blackwater River. Parking for the Gentle Trail is just up the hill on the right, and across the road from a park service area.

WEBSITE: blackwaterfalls.com

WATERWAY: Blackwater River

HEIGHT: 60 feet **CREST:** Varies

NEAREST TOWN: Davis

HIKE DIFFICULTY: Easy

TRAIL QUALITY: Pavement

ROUND-TRIP DISTANCE: 200 yards

ADMISSION: None

TRIP REPORT & TIPS:

Blackwater Falls is one of the highest and most-visited West Virginia waterfalls. And with good reason: the Blackwater River rushes over the ledge in spectacular fashion with a thundering roar that can be deafening during times of high water. Tannic acid from fallen hemlock and red spruce needles leaches into the river, making the water transparent and acidic and making the river look as if it was stained by tea or black coffee. Not everyone will want to tackle the river-level view (page 202), but everyone can view this spectacular waterfall from the Gentle Trail viewing platform. While the view from the Gentle Trail platform is pretty straightforward, it offers a great view. It is my wife's favorite vantage point, and I especially enjoy photographing Blackwater Falls from this spot in the fall and winter.

From the Gentle Trail parking area, follow the short, paved, accessible path through the forest and out to a viewing platform.

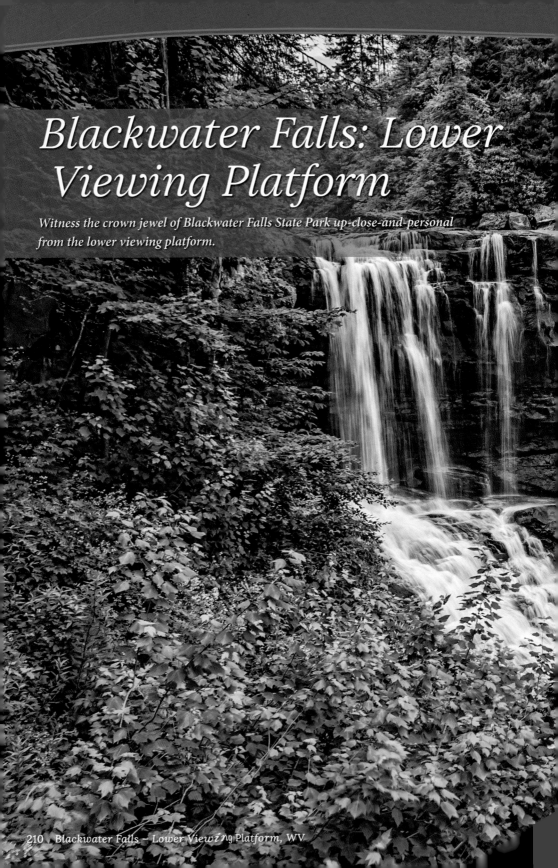

Blackwater Falls: Lower Viewing Platform

Witness the crown jewel of Blackwater Falls State Park up-close-and-personal from the lower viewing platform.

Blackwater Falls: Lower Viewing Platform

This front-row view of the magnificent Blackwater Falls is not to be missed!

LOCATION: Blackwater Falls State Park

ADDRESS/GPS FOR THE FALLS: Trading Post Parking Area; parking area and trail-head: 39° 6.757′ N, 79° 29.023′ W

DIRECTIONS: From the park entrance, continue straight at the stop sign and follow for about 0.2 mile, turn at the second left, and park in the Trading Post Parking Area. The trailhead is signed and obvious.

WEBSITE: blackwaterfalls.com

WATERWAY: Blackwater Falls

HEIGHT: 60 feet **CREST:** Varies

NEAREST TOWN: Davis

HIKE DIFFICULTY: Moderate, with over 200 steps

TRAIL QUALITY: Begins with gravel, then onto a boardwalk

ROUND-TRIP DISTANCE: 0.25 mile

ADMISSION: None

TRIP REPORT & TIPS:

If you want to see Blackwater Falls up close, but aren't particularly fond of the aforementioned (page 202) canyon scramble down to the river, this is the route for you. A series of steps leads you from the Trading Post Parking Area down to a stone patio. From the patio, you'll follow a boardwalk down to a couple of platforms with wonderful views of this West Virginia masterpiece. Be sure to bring your wide-angle lens for great images from the lowest viewing platform. In spring and early summer, you'll be met with blooming flowers along the bank that are perfect foreground complements. You can't go wrong in any season at Blackwater Falls, and especially from this boardwalk system.

Note: Please don't hop the fence here to go down to the river. Save that for the unofficial but established path on the other side of the canyon.

Elakala Falls #1

You'll almost always have an opportunity to capture a swirl here.

Elakala Falls #1

The Falls of Elakala are a series of four waterfalls found on Shays Run, with the first one being the most popular.

LOCATION: Blackwater Falls State Park

ADDRESS/GPS FOR THE FALLS: The Lodge at Blackwater Falls State Park; 39° 6.45′ N, 79° 29.97′ W

DIRECTIONS: From the lodge parking lot, facing the lodge, the trailhead is to your left.

WEBSITE: wvstateparks.com/park/blackwater-falls-state-park/

WATERWAY: Shays Run

HEIGHT: 20 feet **CREST:** Varies

NEAREST TOWN: Davis

HIKE DIFFICULTY: An easy walk from the lodge on the official Elakala Trail, with a moderate scramble down to Shays Run on the unofficial path

TRAIL QUALITY: A nice gravel base on the Elakala Trail; the unofficial path is rife with exposed tree roots and rocks, and is often muddy and slippery

ROUND-TRIP DISTANCE: 0.2 mile

ADMISSION: None

TRIP REPORT & TIPS:

For waterfall photographers, it's hard to top the Falls of Elakala, and especially Elakala #1. Moss-laden rocks and boulders, pretty cascading runs, swirling pools of water, and various lush greenery surround this beautiful waterfall. I've spent many hours here, covering every inch of the stream, making Elakala #1 the most cataloged waterfall in my inventory. This waterfall is always among the favorites of my photography workshop clients as well, and I've received many a high five and seen a lot of happy dances as folks capture their "money shot" of this beauty. Elakala #1 is also my wife's favorite waterfall, and although she doesn't like to fool with a tripod too often, here is where she'll take the time to use one—and she actually has one of the best swirl photos I've seen from here. A visit to Elakala #1 should be on your itinerary whenever you're in the park.

While an image with a dramatic swirl is the shot most photographers are after here, spend a lot of time working other compositions as well. Downstream vantage points should be explored, as there are a couple nice cascades you can place in the foreground. Swirling foam and/or leaves can also be found in a downstream pool and make for a great lead-in to the cascading water in the mid-ground and the waterfall in the background. Although I didn't include it in my image here, the footbridge over Shays Run is a nice feature to use in your frame.

From the trailhead, follow the Elakala Trail as it leads through the woods to a footbridge over Shays Run. Cross the footbridge and continue along the Elakala Trail for 15 yards or so, and look to your right for an unofficial path down to the falls.

Elakala Falls #2

My personal favorite waterfall of the four on Shays Run.

Elakala Falls #2, WV 219

Elkala Falls #2.75

Elakala Falls #2

Although there are several different versions of the legend, the name Elakala comes from Native American lore.

LOCATION: Blackwater Falls State Park

ADDRESS/GPS FOR THE FALLS: The Lodge at Blackwater Falls State Park; 39° 6.464′ N, 79° 29.978′ W

DIRECTIONS: From the lodge parking lot, facing the lodge, the trailhead is to your left.

WEBSITE: wvstateparks.com/park/blackwater-falls-state-park/

WATERWAY: Shays Run

HEIGHT: 18 feet **CREST:** Varies

NEAREST TOWN: Davis

HIKE DIFFICULTY: Moderate scramble down to the base of the falls

TRAIL QUALITY: Fallen trees, exposed roots, and rocks on this spongy unofficial path

ROUND-TRIP DISTANCE: 0.4 mile from the trailhead and back

ADMISSION: None

TRIP REPORT & TIPS:

Elakala #2 is my personal favorite of not only the waterfalls on Shays Run, but of all the waterfalls in the park. The only reason I have more photographs of Elakala #1 is that for a couple years Elakala #2 was not worth photographing, due to several fallen trees marring the scene. When Hurricane Sandy roared through the area in the form of a blizzard, the heavy wet snow toppled trees left and right, and a few of those trees fell on Elakala #2 and in the pool below. Many thanks to several of the park personnel, including then Assistant Park Superintendent Matt Baker (who is now park superintendent), as well as a small group of volunteers who spent a day a few years later cutting out and clearing the trees from the waters along Elakala #2. Not having Elakala #2 at my disposal during that time impressed upon me to always visit and photograph these special places, because at some point, you may find them no longer pristine or accessible.

And speaking of fallen trees, there is one in particular that has rested in the stream since long before Hurricane Sandy; when the water is running over it, it makes for a beautiful foreground, as seen in the image featured here. More moss-covered boulders and rocks highlight the scene on the previous page, and again, plenty of vantage points are available to capture the incredible beauty of this multi-ledged waterfall.

From Elakala #1, continue hiking about 0.1 mile along the unofficial, but obvious, path down to the base of the falls.

Note: While not featured, there are two more waterfalls downstream. Proceed with care if you wish to view them; the last waterfall is particularly difficult to access due to the steep descent and fallen trees.

Upper Falls of Falls Run

LOCATION: Blackwater Falls State Park

ADDRESS/GPS FOR THE FALLS: Gentle Trail Trailhead parking area; 39° 6.732′ N, 79° 28.831′ W

DIRECTIONS: From the Gentle Trail parking area, follow the road in the direction of the lodge and away from the Gentle Trail. In 50 yards or so you'll cross over Falls Run. Continue along the road a bit until you reach an easy way down the bank. Enter the forest and work your way back toward the stream as you gradually descend. In 100 feet 30 yards or so you'll reach the Upper Falls.

WEBSITE: wvstateparks.com/park/blackwater-falls-state-park/

WATERWAY: Falls Run

HEIGHT: 17 feet **CREST:** Varies

NEAREST TOWN: Davis

HIKE DIFFICULTY: Moderate

TRAIL QUALITY: Fair

ROUND-TRIP DISTANCE: 160 yards or so

ADMISSION: None

TRIP REPORT & TIPS:

Falls Run is an extremely small watershed, so you'll have to catch it after tons of rain to make the trek down into the canyon worthwhile. While the Lower Falls of Falls Run is my favorite of the two, I enjoy the Upper Falls too. For straight-on shots or for photos from the opposite bank, you'll have to do some boulder hopping, so be careful. While there is no marked trail here, over the years more and more folks have made the trek, so the path is relatively easy to follow. Be sure to check out a small cascading section of the run a few yards upstream of the Upper Falls, as it's always fun to photograph as well.

Lower Falls of Falls Run

LOCATION: Blackwater Falls State Park

ADDRESS/GPS FOR THE FALLS: Gentle Trail parking area; 39° 6.733′ N, 79° 28.85′ W

DIRECTIONS: From the Upper Falls (featured above), carefully follow the unofficial path for about 40 yards steeply down through the forest, while navigating through rhododendron and over a few boulders.

WEBSITE: wvstateparks.com/park/blackwater-falls-state-park/

WATERWAY: Falls Run

HEIGHT: 25 feet **CREST:** Varies

NEAREST TOWN: Davis

HIKE DIFFICULTY: Strenuous, due to the steep and rocky nature of the path

TRAIL QUALITY: Fair; rhododendron thickets and boulder navigation required

ROUND-TRIP DISTANCE: Around 240 yards from Gentle Trail parking area to Lower Falls and back

ADMISSION: None

TRIP REPORT & TIPS:

When Falls Run is flowing strong, this waterfall is hard to beat. If you're like me, you'll love how the water leaps off the upper ledge onto the various terraced sections of the cliff face. If you're lucky, you'll find yourself in the park during fall foliage season after a couple days of steady rain; the Lower Falls truly shines among the brilliant hues of autumn. Make sure you bring the widest-angle lens you own for this one, as you'll find yourself in a very tight area. Surrounded on both sides by steep hillsides choked with rhododendron and dense forest, you won't have much room to maneuver.

Pendleton Run #2

LOCATION: Blackwater Falls State Park

ADDRESS/GPS FOR THE FALLS: Park Nature Center/Pendleton Lake Area; 39° 6.859′ N, 79° 30.091′ W

DIRECTIONS: From the park entrance, turn right at the stop sign and follow past the campground, and at a junction, bear right to Pendleton Lake and the Nature Center parking area.

WEBSITE: wvstateparks.com/park/blackwater-falls-state-park/

WATERWAY: Pendleton Run

HEIGHT: 12 feet **CREST:** Varies

NEAREST TOWN: Davis

HIKE DIFFICULTY: Easy to moderate

TRAIL QUALITY: Good to fair

ROUND-TRIP DISTANCE: 0.5 mile

ADMISSION: None

TRIP REPORT & TIPS:

Pendleton Run offers several beautiful waterfalls. From the Nature Center parking area, cross the road toward the lake and follow a trail to the left and away from the bike and boat rental building. This path will lead you a short distance through the woods, and then at a small water treatment facility, bear left and follow the trail over the dam and to a small footbridge over the Pendleton Lake spillway. Continue along the trail a short distance to a spur trail to the left. This easy-to-follow trail will lead you down to Pendleton Run. Once you see the creek, work your way a short distance downstream to Pendleton Run #2. The spillway waterfall and Pendleton Run #1, a cascading slide just upstream, aren't pictured here.

Pendleton Run #3

LOCATION: Blackwater Falls State Park

ADDRESS/GPS FOR THE FALLS: Park Nature Center/Pendleton Lake Area; GPS: 39° 6.831′ N, 79° 30.112′ W

DIRECTIONS: From Pendleton Run #2, climb back out of the creek and pick up the trail and follow on downstream. You'll be working your way through some boulders, and then you'll reach a very steep descent, but the path is very easy to follow.

WEBSITE: wvstateparks.com/park/blackwater-falls-state-park/

WATERWAY: Pendleton Run

HEIGHT: 25–30 feet, including a terraced cascade below the main drop **CREST:** Varies

NEAREST TOWN: Davis

HIKE DIFFICULTY: Difficult, due to steep descent, with very few handholds

TRAIL QUALITY: Easy to follow, but rocky, root-strewn and steep

ROUND-TRIP DISTANCE: About 0.6 mile from the Nature Center parking area and back

ADMISSION: None

TRIP REPORT & TIPS:

The terraced cascading water falling all around Pendleton Run #3 makes for interesting compositions. Be sure to explore the many vantage points on either side of the stream. I especially enjoy working my way up the cascade and photographing the main 15-foot drop from the trail side of the stream. Be very careful here as the rocks are quite slippery, and there's nothing but air behind you, so be careful.

Pendleton Run #4

LOCATION: Blackwater Falls State Park

ADDRESS/GPS FOR THE FALLS: Park Nature Center/Pendleton Lake Area; GPS: 39° 6.756′N, 79° 30.142′W

DIRECTIONS: To access Pendleton Run #4 and #5, you can continue following the path you've been on up to this point, but here is where I prefer to work my way down on the other side. I do this because there is a much easier path to follow on the Pendleton Point side of the stream; both sides will be steep, however. Carefully cross Pendleton Run, and pick up a bushwhacked path along the stream, and you'll reach an easy-to-follow gravel path near the Pendleton Point overlook that will lead you down to Pendleton Run #4. If you want to skip the upper two waterfalls and just concentrate on Pendleton Run #3, or only #4 and #5, park at the Pendleton Point overlook and begin your hike here.

WEBSITE: wvstateparks.com/park/blackwater-falls-state-park/

WATERWAY: Pendleton Run

HEIGHT: 20 feet **CREST:** Varies

NEAREST TOWN: Davis

HIKE DIFFICULTY: Strenuous bushwhack through rhododendron and a steep descent

TRAIL QUALITY: Fair

ROUND-TRIP DISTANCE: About 0.7 mile from the Nature Center parking area and back

ADMISSION: None

TRIP REPORT & TIPS:

This is my favorite on Pendleton Run. It's a simple sheer drop, but unlike the other waterfalls on this run, it is situated under a good canopy of lush greens, with moss-covered boulders in the foreground.

Pendleton Run #5

LOCATION: Blackwater Falls State Park

ADDRESS/GPS FOR THE FALLS: Park Nature Center/Pendleton Lake Area; GPS: 39° 6.705′N, 79° 30.177′W

DIRECTIONS: From Pendleton Run #4, follow the gravel trail as it steeply descends to the Blackwater River below. Be careful here, the term *steep* is a bit of an understatement.

WEBSITE: wvstateparks.com/park/blackwaterfalls-state-park/

WATERWAY: Pendleton Run

HEIGHT: About 20 feet, with cascades above and below **CREST:** Varies

NEAREST TOWN: Davis

HIKE DIFFICULTY: Strenuous, due to the very steep nature of the trail

TRAIL QUALITY: Fair, with a lot of loose rock

ROUND-TRIP DISTANCE: About a mile from the Nature Center parking and back

ADMISSION: None

TRIP REPORT & TIPS:

If you made it down to #4, you might as well head on down and not only photograph #5 but also photograph the beautiful and rugged Blackwater River and canyon. As always, take in the many different vantage points available to you here, but also, be very careful on the slippery rocks; the Blackwater River is just below you, and you certainly don't want to be swept away by its swift-moving waters.

Lower Falls
of Hills Creek

At 63 feet, the Lower Falls of Hills Creek is one of West Virginia's highest waterfalls.

Lower Falls of Hills Creek, WV

Lower Falls of Hills Creek

An elaborate system of boardwalks and metal stairs leads you down into the rugged and narrow canyon.

LOCATION: Monongahela National Forest

ADDRESS/GPS FOR THE FALLS: Falls of Hills Creek Scenic Area; 38° 10.392′N, 80° 20.074′W

DIRECTIONS: From the Cranberry Mountain Nature Center, follow WV-39/WV-55 West for 5.4 miles, and turn left onto Hills Creek Falls Road and the parking area.

WEBSITE: tinyurl.com/hillscreekwv

WATERWAY: Hills Creek

HEIGHT: 63 feet **CREST:** Varies

NEAREST TOWN: Hillsboro

HIKE DIFFICULTY: Moderate, due to all the steep steps

TRAIL QUALITY: Good; a mixture of pavement, boardwalks, crushed gravel, and metal steps

ROUND-TRIP DISTANCE: A little under 1.5 miles

ADMISSION: None

TRIP REPORT & TIPS:

I'm doing this one a bit backwards, but due to its sheer beauty, the Lower Falls of Hills Creek deserves top billing. It is actually the last waterfall on the trail, but I want and need to feature it first. The Upper and Middle Falls are listed on pages 232 and 236.

The Falls of Hills Creek Scenic Area is one of the crown jewels in the Monongahela National Forest System crown. Three spectacular waterfalls are hidden in a steep, narrow gorge and surrounded by towering trees and lush greenery. For you flower lovers, visit in the spring and early summer to see over 40 species of wildflowers. This is one of the state's more popular short hikes, and the first 1,700 feet is a fully accessible paved path leading to a viewing platform above the Upper Falls.

The Lower Falls is worthy of a visit during any season, and I'm partial to the spring season when the new greens have emerged on the landscape and Hills Creek is flowing strong. If you can make it here in the winter, you're in for a wonderful sight, as the waterfall often freezes at the base and forms an interesting cone of ice. And of course, fall foliage season is spectacular here, but since this is such a small watershed, you'll need to time your fall visit so that it's after a period of ample rainfall. The viewing platform is ideally placed, offering tremendous views of this West Virginia treasure. Leaving the platform is highly discouraged. You'll notice that some folks have ignored this directive, so if you must leave the platform, please stay on the well-worn path down to the base of the falls; there is simply no need to forge another path through the rare plant life.

From the trailhead at the parking area, follow the paved path to an overlook of the Upper Falls, and continue another 0.5 mile to the Middle Falls, then continue down the boardwalk another 0.25 mile to the Lower Falls viewing platform.

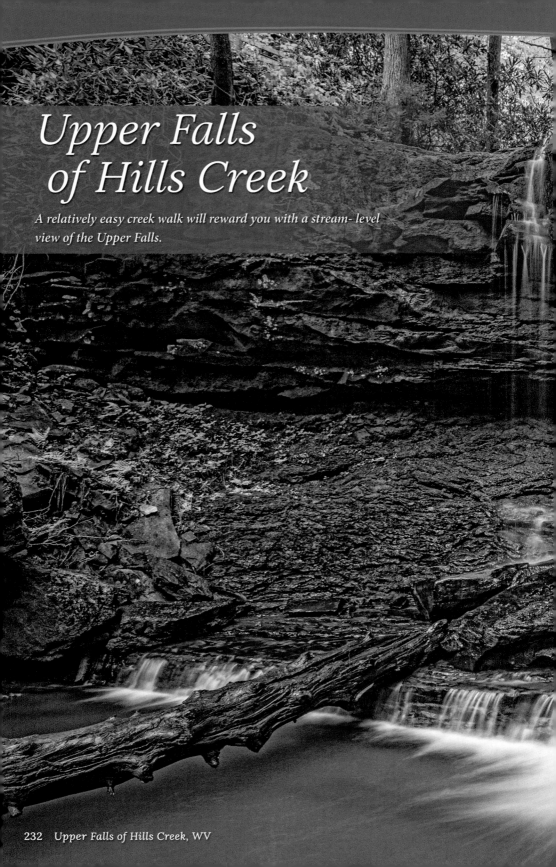

Upper Falls
of Hills Creek

A relatively easy creek walk will reward you with a stream-level view of the Upper Falls.

Upper Falls of Hills Creek, WV 233

Upper Falls of Hills Creek

The Upper Falls viewing platform offers a partial view of the falls—you'll need to get wet to see the falls in all its glory.

LOCATION: Monongahela National Forest

ADDRESS/GPS FOR THE FALLS: Falls of Hills Creek Scenic Area; 38° 10.635′N, 80° 20.205′W

DIRECTIONS: From the Cranberry Mountain Nature Center, follow WV-39/WV-55 West for 5.4 miles, and turn left onto Hills Creek Falls Road and the parking area.

WEBSITE: tinyurl.com/hillscreekwv

WATERWAY: Hills Creek

HEIGHT: 25 feet **CREST:** Varies

NEAREST TOWN: Hillsboro

HIKE DIFFICULTY: Easy to the Upper Falls viewing platform; moderate if you decide to do the creek walk described below

TRAIL QUALITY: A paved path to the viewing platform

ROUND-TRIP DISTANCE: About 0.6 mile to Upper Falls and back

ADMISSION: None

TRIP REPORT & TIPS:

The 1,700-foot paved path offers an accessible means for anyone to catch a glimpse of what Hills Creek has to offer. Unfortunately, the platform doesn't offer a full view of the falls. If you want a better view of the Upper Falls, leave the viewing platform and continue down the trail, which is now a combination of dirt, crushed gravel, and a boardwalk with a series of steps. Once you are level with the stream, it's time to get your feet wet and creek-walk back upstream for that closer view of the Upper Falls. I have been able to rock hop and hug the creek banks, but there are a few sections where you will have to be in the creek. Definitely take a look at the Upper Falls from the observation area before making the creek-walk, though. You don't want to make the effort only to find fallen trees marring the view.

When you're finished at Hills Creek, be sure to check out the Cranberry Glades Botanical Area 6 miles away off of WV-39/WV-55 East. The Glades features a 0.5-mile boardwalk that guides you through bogs typically found in the northern U.S and Canada. Along the boardwalk are tremendous views of the open glades and forest bogs, with numerous unique plants and flowers. Lastly, a visit to the Cranberry Mountain Nature Center is very informative. Located at the junction of WV-150 and WV-39/WV-55, the helpful staff will share information with you about the National Forest and other nearby attractions. You'll also find exhibits featuring the history and wildlife of the area, a small gift shop, and clean restroom facilities.

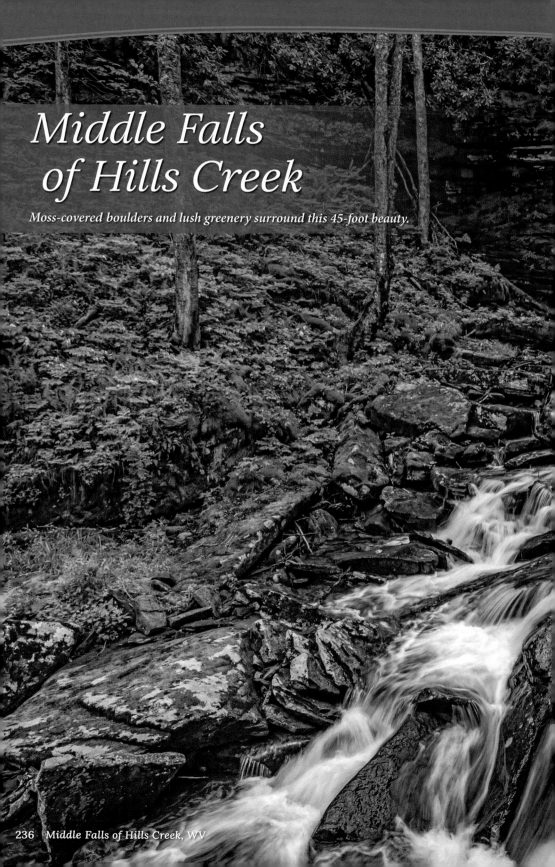

Middle Falls
of Hills Creek

Moss-covered boulders and lush greenery surround this 45-foot beauty.

Middle Falls of Hills Creek, WV   237

Hills Creek

Middle Falls of Hills Creek

Due to the lack of industry and farming around the watershed, Hills Creek is one of the most unspoiled streams in West Virginia.

LOCATION: Monongahela National Forest

ADDRESS/GPS FOR THE FALLS: Falls of Hills Creek Scenic Area; 38° 10.46′ N, 80° 20.118′ W

DIRECTIONS: From the Cranberry Mountain Nature Center, follow WV-39/WV-55 West for 5.4 miles, and turn left onto Hills Creek Falls Road and the parking area.

WEBSITE: tinyurl.com/hillscreekwv

WATERWAY: Hills Creek

HEIGHT: 45 feet **CREST:** Varies

NEAREST TOWN: Hillsboro

HIKE DIFFICULTY: Moderate, due to steps

TRAIL QUALITY: Good; a mixture of pavement, boardwalks, crushed gravel, and metal steps

ROUND-TRIP DISTANCE: 1 mile to Middle Falls and back

ADMISSION: None

TRIP REPORT & TIPS:

The viewing platform places you in a great position for photographing the Middle Falls. You'll be able to work in the foreground boulders for pleasing images. The platform does limit your compositions, though, and you might be tempted to leave the platform for alternate views. This is highly discouraged due to the sensitive nature of the plant life surrounding you. You may be wondering why I mention this while condoning a creek-walk to the Upper Falls. My reply is that in my many trips to the Falls of Hills Creek, I've seen numerous folks fishing along the banks and in the stream between the Upper and Middle Falls. So it is safe to assume that leaving the trail between the two falls is not frowned upon.

From the Upper Falls viewing platform, or from where you entered the stream for a better look at the Upper Falls, continue on down the trail to an upper overlook of the Middle Falls. You won't see much from this vantage point, so continue your journey down an elaborate system of stairs to a short board-walk leading to the lower viewing platform.

Douglas Falls

Douglas Falls is one of my favorite waterfalls and will probably rank very high on your list after you see it in person. But hurry, because seasonal flooding is causing serious erosion and the scene you see here may not be around much longer.

Douglas Falls

While unusually pretty, the reddish-orange rocks here are actually a result of acid mine drainage from old coal mines and coke ovens upstream.

LOCATION: Near Thomas on the Blackwater Canyon Trail

ADDRESS/GPS FOR THE FALLS: At the end of Rail Falls Road in Thomas; 39° 7.427′ N, 79° 31.161′ W

DIRECTIONS: From WV-32 in Thomas, turn onto Douglas Road and follow for 1 mile. Turn left after crossing a bridge over the North Fork Blackwater River and onto the gravel Rail Falls Road. Follow for 1.2 miles until you spot the ample parking and an easy turnaround. The road continues 0.1 mile past this point to a gate, and there is room for a couple cars there, but you run the risk of being blocked in.

WEBSITE: None

WATERWAY: North Fork Blackwater River

HEIGHT: 35 feet **CREST:** Varies

NEAREST TOWN: Thomas

HIKE DIFFICULTY: Moderate, due to loose rocks, a short but steep descent, and uneven terrain

TRAIL QUALITY: Fair

ROUND-TRIP DISTANCE: About 0.2 mile from main parking area and back

ADMISSION: None

TRIP REPORT & TIPS:

Douglas Falls is one of my top-five favorite waterfalls. The setting is amazing, and the compositions are endless. As you make the short but steep descent to the falls, you'll first see an awesome side view of the falls. The path continues downstream, offering several vantage points, and it ends at another steep and rocky descent to the river. From this vantage point, you can feature a wonderful cascade and a scalloped portion of the riverbed as your foreground, with Douglas Falls in the distance.

While the reddish-orange-stained rocks and boulders along the North Fork are unusually pretty, they are a result of an unfortunate man-made disaster. Acid mine drainage from an old upstream coal mine has heavily polluted the river. However, cleanup efforts were put in place and are ongoing, and some aquatic life is beginning to return to the once-dead river. Be careful on these rocks and boulders, as they are extremely slick, even when dry. There are a couple of nice small waterfalls not featured in this book. They begin around 100 yards downstream of Douglas Falls, and access is best gained by going back up to the Blackwater Canyon Trail and walking downstream. The main reason I haven't included these two waterfalls is that they are choked with fallen trees and not very photoworthy at this point in time. Perhaps in a few years, they'll be free of the trees, and worth the crazy-steep scramble down. But, there is one downstream waterfall you must check out if you're up for an adventure; see page 248 for details. Lastly, on your drive back out, give Albert Falls (page 263) a quick look. It's always a fun little waterfall to photograph.

High Falls of the Cheat

A gorgeous waterfall in a true backcountry setting.

High Falls of the Cheat

Take a hike or ride an excursion train to this beautiful waterfall in the Monongahela National Forest Backcountry.

LOCATION: Monongahela National Forest

ADDRESS/GPS FOR THE FALLS: High Falls Trailhead/Beulah Road; 38° 46.333′ N, 79° 46.65′ W

DIRECTIONS: From Alpena, on US-33 (about 13 miles east of Elkins and 10.5 miles west of Harman) turn onto Glady Road (County Road 27), and follow for about 9.6 miles to Glady. Turn left onto Bemis Road and follow for 0.2 mile, and turn right onto Beulah Road (Forest Road 44). Follow for 3.9 miles to parking on the right. The trailhead is about 75 yards up the road.

WEBSITE: No website for the waterfall itself, but if you're interested in the excursion train, check out the following link and select the New Tygart Flyer: mountainrailwv.com/

WATERWAY: Shavers Fork of the Cheat River

HEIGHT: 15 feet **CREST:** Varies

NEAREST TOWN: Glady

HIKE DIFFICULTY: Strenuous, unless you ride the excursion train!

TRAIL QUALITY: Fair with soggy, marshy areas and ankle-turning rocks

ROUND-TRIP DISTANCE: Around 8.4 miles

ADMISSION: None, unless you ride the train

TRIP REPORT & TIPS:

Access to this backcountry waterfall is surprisingly easy if you choose to take the excursion train out of Elkins. Our little girl Hannah is fascinated by "choo-choos," so we opted to take her on the train ride one summer day. She was not yet two at that time, but she had a great time and loved the waterfall.

If you prefer the solitude of hiking, the High Falls Trail is for you. From the trail-head, follow the blue diamond–blazed High Falls Trail for 0.2 mile, and cross a footbridge spanning the West Fork River. In about 0.3 mile the High Falls trail will join the Allegheny Trail at an old access road. Cross the access road, and pass through a large field, as the now blue/yellow-blazed Allegheny/High Falls Trail climbs Shaver Mountain. In 1.2 miles from the field, arrive at the saddle on Shaver Mountain and a good-looking campsite. Just past the campsite, arrive at the intersection where the Allegheny Trail splits left. Stay straight, now going downhill on the blue-blazed High Falls Trail, and reach a small abandoned service road in 0.2 mile. Turn right and follow the service road for another 0.2 mile, where the High Falls Trail turns left off of the service road downhill. Follow the blue-blazed High Falls Trail for 1.1 miles, arriving at the railroad tracks. Turn right, and follow beside the railroad tracks for 0.9 mile to High Falls. Pay extra attention for trains, and don't walk in the middle of the tracks.

No matter how you arrive to High Falls, you'll be blown away by its beauty. Its horseshoe shape offers many composition choices, such as the rocky bank below the pool area, and a cascading downstream area.

Kennedy Falls

LOCATION: Blackwater Canyon Trail

ADDRESS/GPS FOR THE FALLS: Downstream of Douglas Falls on the Blackwater Canyon Trail; 39° 7.218′ N, 79° 31.221′ W

DIRECTIONS: From WV-32 in Thomas, turn onto Douglas Road and follow for 1 mile. Turn left after crossing a bridge over the North Fork Blackwater River, onto the gravel Rail Falls Road. Follow for 1.2 miles for ample parking and an easy turnaround. The road continues past this point for another 0.1 mile to a gate, and there is room for a couple cars there, but you run the risk of being blocked in.

WEBSITE: None

WATERWAY: North Fork Blackwater River

HEIGHT: 30 feet **CREST:** Varies

NEAREST TOWN: Thomas

HIKE DIFFICULTY: An easy walk from the gate above Douglas Falls, then a strenuous descent into the canyon

TRAIL QUALITY: Good until the descent, then the "path" becomes steep, with loose rocks and soil

ROUND-TRIP DISTANCE: Around 1 mile

ADMISSION: None

TRIP REPORT & TIPS:

From the gate near Douglas Falls, continue following the Blackwater Canyon Trail downstream for around 0.25 mile. Look for a scattering of old railroad ties along the bank and a drainage; begin your descent into the canyon here, then work your way to the drainage and follow it down to the river above Kennedy Falls.

Once you reach the river, you'll pick up a relatively easy-to-follow path along the river and down to the base of the falls. There's a rather difficult section to navigate near the base, and while I haven't used rope to aid in my descent, if you have it, you might want to bring it. It's a tricky route along a very narrow section of the steep hillside, with only some exposed tree roots to offer a stabilizing handhold. When you're at the river, you'll notice the rocks are stained here, just like they are upstream at Douglas Falls. You'll also notice they're just as slick, so be very careful.

Upper Falls of Big Run

LOCATION: Monongahela National Forest

ADDRESS/GPS FOR THE FALLS: Forest Road 18; 39° 6.433′N, 79° 34.121′W

DIRECTIONS: From Thomas, follow US-219 South toward Parsons. At around 6 miles, you'll pass Tucker County High School; continue for around 0.5 mile, and watch closely for a left turn onto Forest Road 18. Take it and follow a short distance, and at a junction, turn left and follow for a little over 2 miles to an obvious campsite. If you continue straight, you'll reach Olson Tower, which offers a beautiful panoramic view of the area.

WEBSITE: None

WATERWAY: Big Run

HEIGHT: 15 feet **CREST:** Varies

NEAREST TOWN: Thomas

HIKE DIFFICULTY: Moderate, due to a couple short boulder hops and a soggy, muddy section near the falls

TRAIL QUALITY: Fair, with some exposed roots and a few muddy spots

ROUND-TRIP DISTANCE: 200 yards

ADMISSION: None

TRIP REPORT & TIPS:

I love everything about this little waterfall. It is in a beautiful sheltered area surrounded by rhododendron and mountain laurel. Many thanks to my friends Donna and Rabbit for leading me here several years ago.

Walk down the road 50 yards or so from where you parked, and look for a drainage to your right and follow down a few feet, then bear left following the obvious path down to the falls. There are two more waterfalls here. They're very obvious and right behind you. The first is a 6-foot cascade, and the next is a drop of around 15–20 feet. You can carefully work your way down and photograph the 6-footer from where you're standing. The best way to view the lower fall is to go back up the path a short distance and look for a bush-whacked trail through the rhododendron forest. My friend Brian Peterman has worked hard to get this path navigable. I wouldn't make the trek through here, though, unless you're there when Big Run is flowing strong; the shots of the lower falls just aren't worth the effort during times of low water.

More West Virginia Falls

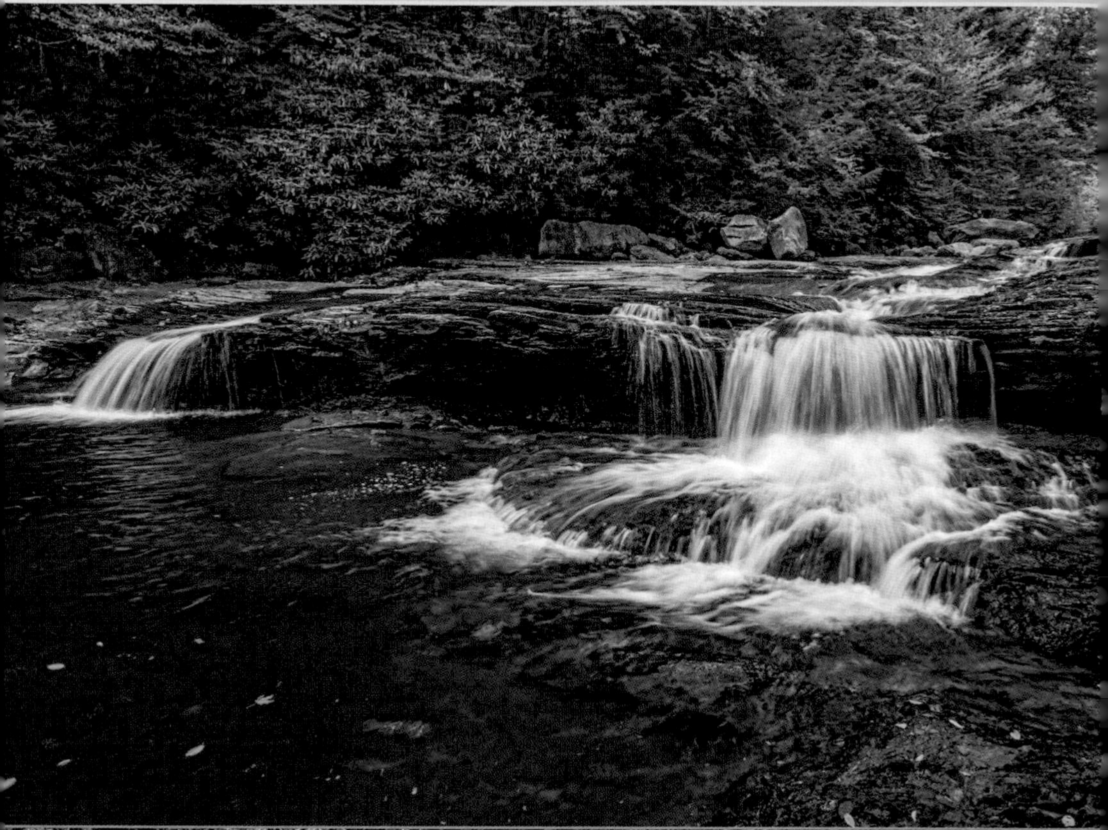

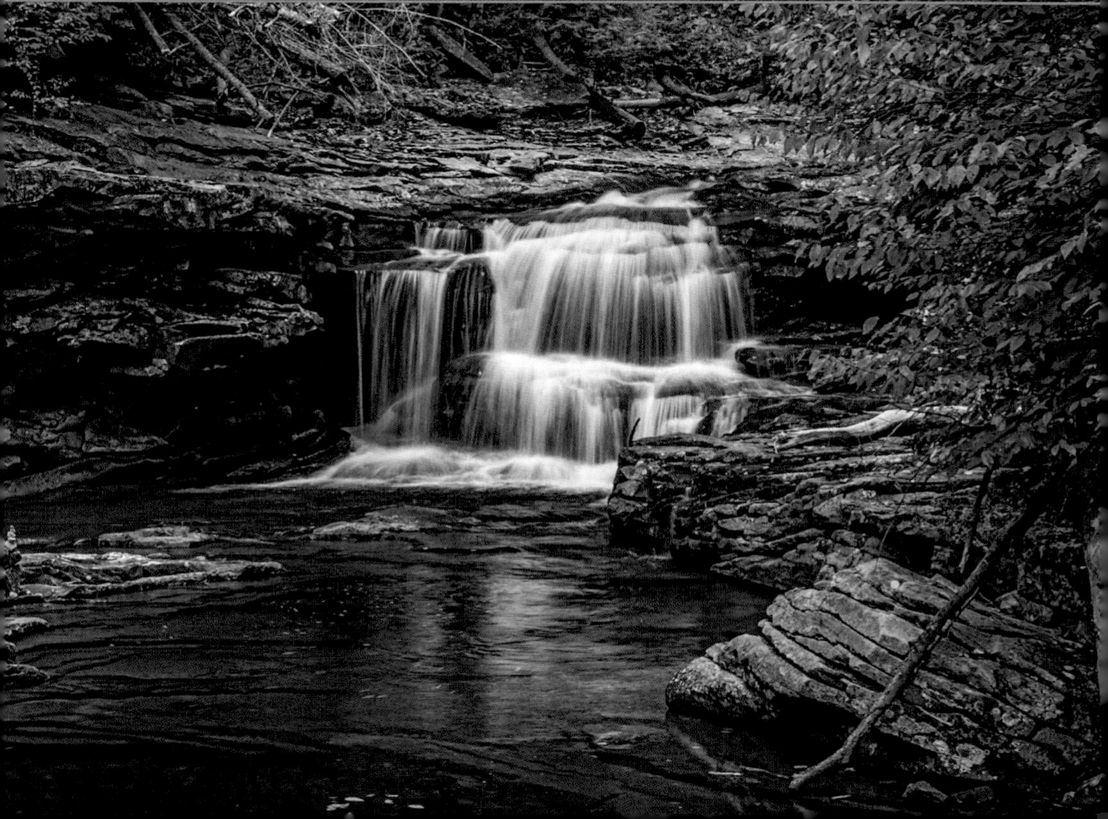

Lower Red Creek Falls

LOCATION: Monongahela National Forest/Dolly Sods Wilderness

ADDRESS/GPS FOR THE FALLS: Forest Road 75; 38° 59'43.19" N, 79° 21.31' W

DIRECTIONS: From Laneville, cross the bridge over Red Creek, and follow Forest Road 19 for 3.8 miles, then bear left onto Forest Road 75 for 3 miles to the parking area on the left for the Fisher Spring Run Trailhead.

WEBSITE: None

WATERWAY: Red Creek

HEIGHT: 7 feet **CREST:** Varies

NEAREST TOWN: Laneville

HIKE DIFFICULTY: Moderate to strenuous

TRAIL QUALITY: Very rocky, with exposed roots

ROUND-TRIP DISTANCE: 4.2 miles

ADMISSION: None

TRIP REPORT & TIPS:

I chose to feature these two waterfalls on the main stream of Red Creek. There are several routes to the waterfalls here, but I'll detail the route I chose to follow. From the Fisher Spring Run Trailhead on Forest Road 75, follow the trail down through the forest for 1.2 miles to the Rohrbaugh Trail. Turn right and follow the old railroad grade to the 1.7-mile mark, then bear left and head downhill along a series of switchbacks. At the 1.9-mile mark, cross Fisher Spring Run and head uphill a bit to cross another section of the stream. At around the 2.1-mile mark, you will be above Red Creek, and you should be able to make out a spur path down to camping spots. Once there, you'll be near the top of Lower Red Creek Falls.

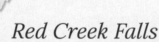

Red Creek Falls

LOCATION: Monongahela National Forest/Dolly Sods Wilderness

ADDRESS/GPS FOR THE FALLS: Forest Road 75; 38° 59.868' N, 79° 21.347' W

DIRECTIONS: From Laneville, cross the bridge over Red Creek, and follow Forest Road 19 for 3.8 miles, then bear left onto Forest Road 75 for 3 miles to the parking area on the left for the Fisher Spring Run Trailhead.

WEBSITE: None

WATERWAY: Red Creek

HEIGHT: 15 feet **CREST:** Varies

NEAREST TOWN: Laneville

HIKE DIFFICULTY: Moderate to strenuous

TRAIL QUALITY: Very rocky, with exposed roots

ROUND-TRIP DISTANCE: 4.8 miles

ADMISSION: None

TRIP REPORT & TIPS:

I'd like to thank my friends Anne Johnson and Dave Miller for their updates on the waterfalls in Dolly Sods. Dave had alerted me to a few downed trees at Red Creek Falls, but I wasn't prepared for a party of three camping near the base of the falls. These obstacles impeded my composition options, but it was great to see the falls again.

From Lower Red Creek Falls, follow Red Creek upstream for 0.3 mile. The spur path will lead you through the camp sites and eventually deposit you at the creek, where you'll need to rock-hop across Fisher Spring Run to the falls. To complete your trip, backtrack to Lower Red Creek Falls and pick up the trail back to the trailhead.

Valley Falls

LOCATION: Valley Falls State Park

ADDRESS/GPS FOR THE FALLS: Parking Area at the end of Valley Falls Road; 26554; 39° 23.186′ N, 80° 5.218′ W

DIRECTIONS: From I-79 in Fairmont, take exit 137 and follow WV-310 South for 7.8 miles. Turn right onto Valley Falls Road, and follow 2.8 miles to the park.

WEBSITE: tinyurl.com/valleyfallswv

WATERWAY: Tygart Valley River

HEIGHT: 25 feet **CREST:** Varies

NEAREST TOWN: Fairmont

HIKE DIFFICULTY: Easy

TRAIL QUALITY: Pavement and gravel

ROUND-TRIP DISTANCE: 0.2 mile

ADMISSION: None

TRIP REPORT & TIPS:

River-wide waterfalls are hard to beat, and here at Valley Falls, you get the added benefit of some great downriver scenes with awesome boulders and rapids in your foreground. When the water is up, it's quite impressive to see the water flying by and crashing over the 350-foot-wide ledge and then narrowing down into about a 165-foot-wide section. But, I really like Valley Falls when the water is lower, so you can move about more freely along the river and see more segments of the waterfalls. Be sure to check out Twin Falls (page 256) while you're here, because it's a beauty.

Valley Falls State Park is in an area that was once a grist and lumber mill community, with a few historic remnants scattered around the park. Valley Falls is a day-use park, and the road is gated from sunset to sunrise, so plan accordingly.

From the parking area, cross a bridge over an active railroad line, and then follow the path down to the falls.

Twin Falls

LOCATION: Valley Falls State Park

ADDRESS/GPS FOR THE FALLS: Rhododendron Trail; 39° 24.127′ N, 80° 5.71′ W

DIRECTIONS: From I-79 in Fairmont, take exit 137 and follow WV-310 South for 7.8 miles. Turn right onto Valley Falls Road, and follow 2.8 miles to the park. The Rhododendron Trailhead is at the western end of the parking area.

WEBSITE: None

WATERWAY: Glady Creek

HEIGHT: 20 feet **CREST:** Varies

NEAREST TOWN: Fairmont

HIKE DIFFICULTY: Easy

TRAIL QUALITY: Wide dirt path

ROUND-TRIP DISTANCE: 1.9 miles

ADMISSION: None

TRIP REPORT & TIPS:

I met up with my good friends Mike and Cheryl one fine spring day for the quick hike to Twin Falls. For years I'd seen some great images on social media posts by several friends and contacts, but the trip with Mike and Cheryl was my first time to this beauty. I was glad to finally see this remarkable waterfall, but I also kicked myself for taking so long to get here. If you've not been here yet, don't delay any longer. You'll love this spectacular waterfall.

Note: Time your visit in the spring or after periods of ample rain. An upstream lake holds back the waters of Glady Creek, so during the dryer months, Twin Falls has little water flowing over the ledge.

From the western end of the parking area, follow the Rhododendron Trail for about 1 mile. You'll encounter a few trail junctions, but always bear left and stay parallel to the railroad line and river below. Near Glady Creek, the trail will veer to the right and begin climbing up the mountain. There is an obvious spur trail to the left that takes you down to the creek, and then it veers right to follow the creek upstream a very short distance to the falls. Mike and I had to wade through knee-high water to get to the vantage points we preferred, but there are several areas you can shoot from that won't require getting wet.

Big Cove Run

LOCATION: In Barbour County about 30 minutes from Philippi

ADDRESS/GPS FOR THE FALLS: Cove Run Road; 39° 14.733′ N, 79° 56.083′ W

DIRECTIONS: From Philippi, follow US-250 South for 3 miles, then take WV-38 East for 6.3 miles. Turn left onto WV-92 North, and follow for 5.9 miles, then turn left onto Cove Run Road/County Road 2 (Google lists this road as Coal Run Road). At around 0.8 mile, bear right to stay on Cove Run Road, and in about a mile at a "T" intersection bear right. Follow for a short distance, and then bear left and follow for a little over 1 mile to a pulloff on the left.

WEBSITE: None

WATERWAY: Big Cove Run

HEIGHT: 15 feet **CREST:** Varies

NEAREST TOWN: Philippi

HIKE DIFFICULTY: Moderate, due to some scrambling down to the creek

TRAIL QUALITY: Fair, due to some off-trail scrambling

ROUND-TRIP DISTANCE: Around 100 yards

ADMISSION: None

TRIP REPORT & TIPS:

The Upper Falls of Big Cove Run is a neat little waterfall with an interesting flow pattern.

From the pulloff, cross Big Cove Run on a concrete bridge, then enter the woods and scramble down to the base of the falls. This is a fun waterfall to photograph, with several interesting vantage points available. About 0.2 mile down the road, and in sight of the river/lake, is the Lower Falls of Big Cove Run.

Arden Falls (Moats Falls)

LOCATION: Near Philippi in Barbour County

ADDRESS/GPS FOR THE FALLS: County Road 12/8; 39° 12.326′ N, 79° 57.54′ W

DIRECTIONS: From Philippi, follow US-119 N/US-250 N for around 4.3 miles, and turn right onto County Road 6/Arden Road. Follow to a junction and bear right, staying on County Road 6, and follow to another junction, and again bear right, onto what is now County Road 12. Follow a short distance, and after crossing the bridge spanning the Tygart Valley River, turn left and follow for about 2.1 miles.

WEBSITE: None

WATERWAY: Tygart Valley River

HEIGHT: 15 feet **CREST:** Varies

NEAREST TOWN: Arden

HIKE DIFFICULTY: Easy scramble from roadside

TRAIL QUALITY: Good, with a little bit of boulder hopping required

ROUND-TRIP DISTANCE: A few yards

ADMISSION: None

TRIP REPORT & TIPS:

There's so much to take in here at Arden Falls, and I'm looking forward to a return visit. Knowing that this area has had an unfortunate number of drowning deaths, we carefully made our way along the various boulders and rocks and steered relatively clear of the swift-moving, dangerous current.

Note: This area is very popular/rowdy in summer and on weekends. You might want to steer clear during those times.

Matador Falls

LOCATION: Bull Run Road–Cheat Canyon

ADDRESS/GPS FOR THE FALLS: 39° 35.549′ N, 79° 45.548′ W

DIRECTIONS: From Masontown, follow Herring Road/County Road 23 east for 0.8 mile. Turn left onto Bull Run Road/County Road 21 and follow for 3.4 miles to a pullout on the left.

WEBSITE: None

WATERWAY: Bull Run

HEIGHT: 15 feet **CREST:** Varies

NEAREST TOWN: Masontown

HIKE DIFFICULTY: Moderate, due to steep scramble

TRAIL QUALITY: Easy-to-follow dirt path, then a short bushwhack through rhododendron and boulders

ROUND-TRIP DISTANCE: 150 yards

ADMISSION: None

TRIP REPORT & TIPS:

The rugged Cheat River Canyon is an area that I've just started to explore. This waterfall on Bull Run was brought to my attention by a few photographer friends, and it's been high on my list ever since. I made a quick trip here with my buddy Mike after a day of heavy rain. Slippery conditions coupled with high water made the compositions a bit challenging, but it was still a lot of fun. Be careful along the stream: the rocks are extremely slick.

From the pullout, walk back up the road a short distance, and you'll notice a path leading down to the stream. Follow this path about 50 yards, and then on the final 25 yards down to the creek, you'll have to duck through some rhododendron before reaching the stream.

Lower Falls of Deckers Creek

LOCATION: Roadside park along WV-7

ADDRESS/GPS FOR THE FALLS: WV-7; 39° 33′54.22″ N, 79° 49.378′ W

DIRECTIONS: From I-68 in Morgantown, take exit 4 and follow WV-7 East for around 8 miles to the roadside park on the right.

WEBSITE: None

WATERWAY: Deckers Creek

HEIGHT: A segmented drop of around 12 feet

CREST: Varies

NEAREST TOWN: Masontown

HIKE DIFFICULTY: Moderate scramble

TRAIL QUALITY: Dirt path with loose rocks and exposed roots, then a slide down the ledge and onto boulders

ROUND-TRIP DISTANCE: 100 yards

ADMISSION: None

TRIP REPORT & TIPS:

I first learned of Deckers Creek via a book on West Virginia Whitewater. But it wasn't until seeing some great shots from my friends Brian, Rick, and Bobbie that I became serious about checking out the place. There are three waterfalls in a relatively short section of the stream; I opted to feature the last one of them here.

To access this waterfall, follow the well-worn path at the lower end of the park down to the creek, and then carefully slide down a slanted boulder to reach the base of the falls. To reach the other two waterfalls, follow a path along the guardrail on the upper section of the park to another path that leads down to the stream—you can't miss the paths, or the falls.

12 More West Virginia Waterfalls to Explore

	GPS Coordinates	Location	Height
	Drawdy Falls 38° 8.031' N 81° 41.322' W	Drawdy Falls Roadside Park near Peytona on WV-3 in Boone County.	Two drops, both around 5 feet each
	Lick Creek Falls 37° 47.054' N 80° 53.454' W	Roadside along WV-20 near Sandstone. A nice cascading stream section is found upstream.	8 feet
	Chapel Falls 37° 37.646' N 81° 1.156' W	Beside the Rhoda Ann Memorial Church in Streeter, WV.	5 feet
	Hemlock Hollow Falls 37° 52.708' N 80° 58.365' W	About 6.5 miles north of the Prince train station via WV-41 north.	20 feet
	Meadow Fork Falls 37° 56.656' N 81° 5.506' W	New River Gorge National River—access is via an old jeep road about 0.5 mile downstream of Dunloup Creek Falls (page 152).	7 feet
	Coal Run Falls 38° 0.05' N 81° 2.023' W	New River Gorge National River—across the road from Brooklyn Mine Trailhead Parking in the Cunard River Access Area.	20 feet

	GPS Coordinates	Location	Height
	Propps Ridge Falls 38° 6.626' N 80° 55.676' W	About 4.5 miles from Lookout on Propps Ridge Road.	15 feet
	Westlake Falls 38° 7.905' N 81° 6.005' W	Near the beginning of the Ansted-Hawks Nest Rail Trail. Check out the remnants of the old mill house.	15 feet
	Upper Mill Creek Falls 38° 7.914' N 81° 5.983' W	Near the beginning of the Ansted-Hawks Nest Rail Trail and within eyesight of Westlake Falls (pictured above).	8 feet
	Flatwoods Run 38° 49.273' N 80° 20.307' W	Kanawha Run Road, just off of WV-20 in Upsher County.	A 7-foot drop followed by a cascading run
	Albert Falls 39° 7.711' N 79° 31.222' W	Rail Falls Road—about 0.4 mile upstream from Douglas Falls (page 240).	9 feet
	Elklick Run Falls 39° 1.183' N 79° 31.614' W	About 8.5 miles from Hendricks via WV-72 South and River Road.	10 feet

10 More Tips

1. Pre-Trip Planning–Before your waterfall trips, consult weather forecasts for predicted rainfall and cloud cover percentages, as well as historical data on how much rain has fallen recently. This should give you a good barometer for knowing if the waterfalls you're visiting will have enough water flow and cloud coverage for great photos.

The Photographer's Ephemeris and similar desktop or smartphone apps are great tools and show you where and when the sun will be in specific places at specific times. You'll be able to adequately plan a waterfall shoot on cloudless days by seeing how long you'll have in a certain place before the sunlight hits the water. You can also use the Time Slider on Google Earth to show sunlight across the landscape. For instance, on my Scott's Run shoot in Northern Virginia, I knew I was going to be there on a day with no cloud cover. So, before leaving on the trip, I used *The Photographer's Ephemeris* to see the angle of the sun over Scott's Run, and I used the Time Slider on Google Earth to approximate when the waterfall would be out of the shadows. With these tools, I knew that I should photograph the waterfall before 9:30 am on the morning of my visit. I arrived there at 8:45 am, and the photograph used for this book was made at 9:06 am.

2. Extra Clothing–Always have extra clothes with you, even for quick day trips. In my vehicle at all times is a full set of extra clothes, adjusted seasonally. I also always have extra hiking boots/shoes, a raincoat and rain pants, a blanket, and a couple towels. It pays to be prepared when chasing waterfalls.

3. Random Gear–I'm not a big gear or gadget junkie, but there are a couple items that I use frequently when chasing waterfalls. When wading into or crossing a stream, or even just walking along a creek bank, you'll be encountering very slick conditions. Traction cleats that slip over your boots are a fantastic piece of gear that help you maintain control while walking in or around the creeks. I use STREAMtrekkers, but there are other good ones out there. I ran into a social media contact a couple years ago, and he showed me his version of traction control. He simply screwed short sheet metal screws into the soles of his boots, and the heads of the screws gave him the traction he needed. In winter, I use the YakTrax Summit style due to their 3/8th-inch spikes that help me maintain traction in snow and ice.

I mention "getting wet" or "creek-walking" often throughout this book. When the water is not ice cold, I will get in the creek with my close-toed water shoes with the traction device attached. If I'm on a long hike, I'll simply tether the water shoes and traction device to my pack so I'll have them with me, or if there are a lot of stream crossings, I'll just get my hiking boots wet and utilize an extra pair of dry boots and socks when I get back to my vehicle. When the water is extremely cold, I'll wade around the creek in muck boots with the traction device attached. If I know the water will be higher than my muck boots, I'll use my hip waders.

4. **More Random Gear**–Be sure to bring along spare memory cards, extra charged batteries, as well as a backup camera, even if it's a point and shoot. I also carry a power inverter in my vehicle, so I can charge batteries as needed while on the road.

5. **Work with the Sun**–Catch the sun bursting through trees by using a narrow aperture such as f13–f22, and shoot directly into the sun. A sunburst in your frame will give the image a unique look.

6. **Embrace the Weather**–Don't put your gear away when the weather isn't the greatest. Beautiful waterfall images can be made in the winter, with ice and snow creating interest. Shooting during a light rain or just after a rain shower is perfect to obtain even light throughout the scene, and all the surfaces will be wet; just be sure to rotate the outer ring of your circular polarizing filter to eliminate the glare found on the wet rocks and surroundings.

7. **Magnify for Optimum Focus**–If your camera has Live View, use the magnifying button to zoom in on a background object to ensure proper manual or automatic focus. Also, this will assist you as you rotate your circular polarizing filter to achieve the desired effect.

8. **RAW**–If you're not already doing so, shoot your images in RAW format so that you can get much more out of your photos in postprocessing. If you're uncomfortable with or new to processing RAW files, you can shoot in RAW+-JPEG, and you'll have the RAW files at your disposal when you're ready to learn more about processing RAW files.

9. Backup, Backup, Backup–Backup your photos online and/or via external hard drives, and have at least one external hard drive stored off-site. Don't rely on just one external hard drive, though, as they are prone to crashes.

10. Stay Clean–Keep your lenses and filters clean; wipe them with lens cloths or lens cleaners early and often. Shooting around waterfalls will guarantee a stray water spot or two, and it's much easier to continuously clean your filters and lenses in the field than it is to try to remove water spots in postprocessing.

Have fun and be safe!

Virginia Waterfalls Checklist

Blue Ridge Parkway and Vicinity

Shenandoah National Park

Piedmont Region

Northern Virginia

West Virginia Waterfalls Checklist

Upper New River Gorge and Bluestone River Tributaries

Central New River Gorge

Lower New River Gorge and Gauley River Tributaries

About the Author

I am a West Virginia–based landscape photographer. Through my photography, my ultimate desire is to glorify God's creation and showcase the natural beauty of West Virginia, and inspire others to preserve and protect the many special places found in the Mountain State.

For over 20 years I have been traipsing about West Virginia in search of grand vistas, majestic waterfalls, and intimate forest scenes. I spend most of my time exploring and photographing the amazingly beautiful scenery found in the New River Gorge National River, the Monongahela National Forest, the Canaan Valley National Wildlife Refuge, and the various state parks and wildlife management areas throughout the state.

I am coauthor of the multi-award-winning book *West Virginia Waterfalls: The New River Gorge*. I conduct photography workshops throughout West Virginia and beyond. My images have appeared in print and digital publications (both regional and national), are in private and corporate collections, and have been used for marketing and corporate recruitment. I work with several advertising/marketing agencies, with duties ranging from capturing specific images for various publications to covering events like the National Boy Scout Jamboree, and I was photographer in residence for the Canaan Valley National Wildlife Refuge. I am a juried fine arts photographer with Tamarack: The Best of West Virginia, located in Beckley, and my work can also be viewed at the Buxton and Landstreet Gallery in Thomas, WV. I reside in Williamson with my wife Melissa, our daughter Hannah, and my trusty hiking companion Rocky, our mixed-breed dog.

To order prints, see the results of his latest photography trips and more, visit www.randallsanger.com.